Autograph of
Paramahamsa Nithyananda

Published by

LIFE BLISS FOUNDATION

&

NITHYANANDA VEDIC SCIENCES UNIVERSITY PRESS (NVSU)
· A division of Nithyananda Vedic Sciences University, USA

The meditation techniques included in this book are to be practiced only after personal instructions by an ordained teacher of Life Bliss Foundation (LBF) or Nithyananda Vedic Sciences University (NVSU). If some one tries these techniques without prior participation in the meditation programs of LBF or NVSU, they shall be doing so entirely at their own risk; neither the author nor LBF nor NVSU shall be responsible for the consequences of their actions.

ISBN 10: 1-934364-07-X   ISBN 13: 978-1-934364-07-9
Copyright© 2008
First Edition: Dec 2005
Second Edition: May 2008

All rights reserved. No part of this publication may be reproduced, or stored in a retrieval system, or transmitted by any form or by any means, electronic, mechanical, photocopying, recording or otherwise, without written permission of the publisher. In the event that you use any of the information in this publication for yourself, the author and the publisher assume no responsibility for your actions.

All proceeds from the sale of this book go towards supporting charitable activities.
Printed in India by WQ Judge Press, Bangalore, Tel. : +91 80 22211168

*Discourses delivered to Swamis and Ananda Samajis
of the Nithyananda Order all over the world.*

YOU ARE NO SINNER!

Paramahamsa Nithyananda

Published by
LIFE BLISS FOUNDATION
&
NITHYANANDA VEDIC SCIENCES UNIVERSITY PRESS (NVSU)
A division of Nithyananda Vedic Sciences University, USA

Contents

Guilt, The Sure Killer Of Intelligence   7

Love To Survive   31

Lifestyle Is Not Life   49

Life Is An Eternal Celebration   67

Trust — Even If You Are Exploited   85

From Subconsciousness To Superconsciousness   101

Fall In To Rise   123

Lust To Love   145

Guilt,
The Sure Killer Of Intelligence

L*et me start with a small story:*

In a small village, a little away from the main living area, the temple priest lived with his family. He was a pious man and his whole life, he spent in taking care of the local deity. He would bathe the deity, decorate it with fresh flowers and do the daily puja - offering. All the villagers respected him and his family.

One rainy night, just after dinner when the priest was relaxing with his family, he heard a knock on the door. Someone was knocking rather urgently. The priest was puzzled as no one from the village would come at that time of the night to his house. He opened the door and was totally surprised to see a young woman standing, completely soaked in the rain. The woman looked beautiful and well dressed.

She asked the priest, 'Please, can I stay here tonight? I was traveling to the next town when I got caught in the pouring rain. Tomorrow morning I will be gone. I will leave this place.'

The priest did not know what to do. He called his wife and informed her of the situation. The wife saw the poor woman standing and shivering outside. Being a compassionate woman she immediately asked her to come in, gave her dry clothes to wear, some hot food to eat and a warm bed to sleep in.

The next day morning, the woman thanked her hosts for their generosity and was about to take leave. As she was standing, waiting for the horse-carriage to arrive, the priest and his wife started talking casually to her. They said to her, 'In India we don't hesitate to ask about each other and share personal information.

'Who are you? Where are you from?'

The woman replied, 'I am the king's favourite courtesan. My mother has taken ill suddenly, so I am on my way to my mother's place.' At that very moment the carriage arrived and she left.

The priest and his wife were very disturbed. They thought, 'What a big sin we have committed by giving shelter and food to a courtesan.'

They immediately ran towards the well and drew water from it to clean the whole house! They burnt the bed she had slept in and then had a complete head bath to wash away the sin of sheltering a courtesan in their house that was filled with pictures of all the Gods.

They felt so guilty that they even went up to the temple deity and wept, 'Oh God, please forgive us for the sin of giving food and shelter to a woman of loose morals. Even if we did it for a single night, we are guilty of sinning against you! Please forgive us.'

Suddenly the priest heard a voice from heaven. The voice was also weeping. The priest and his wife were surprised. The priest asked, 'Who is that who is weeping?'

From above the voice came again, 'I am God. I am weeping.' The priest was shaken. He asked, 'But why are You weeping?' God replied, 'You have given shelter to a courtesan for one night and you think that it is a big sin. I give food and shelter to her everyday and for many others like her! Where will I go and wash my sins? That is why I am weeping.'

There is a beautiful moral to be understood from this story. The priest and his wife thought that they were holier than the courtesan. They offered her a place to stay out of a superior feeling, not out of compassion. It was their ego that played up.

All our guilt, all our rules, all our morality, all our ideas of right and wrong, are created only by these types of priests. When I say this, I mean the type of people who think they are holier than others; whose morality is confined to the skin level; who think they are more pure than others; that they are greater than others for no real reason except that they are priests. They are responsible for creating the rules which create guilt in us.

According to me, guilt is the greatest sin that we can commit. For our other sins, we will be punished only after our death. The sin of guilt punishes us while we live.

Look a little deeper. What is the root cause of guilt? It is our idea about right and wrong - our understanding about what is right and what is wrong. That is where guilt starts. What is right? What is wrong? Let us analyze. What is the scale to measure right or wrong?

In Hinduism, vegetarianism is right; in Christianity non-vegetarianism is right. In Hinduism you can marry only once; in Islam you can marry four times. In Hinduism, you can't drink alcohol; in Christianity, wine is part of worship. There are so many rules, so many regulations, different in different places, different in different situations and in different societies.

For somebody, a particular food might be *amrita* (nectar), while for another person the same thing might be poison!

In South India, fish is considered to be non-vegetarian food. But in West Bengal, they refer to fish as *Gangaphal* (fruit from the sacred river Ganga!). Bengali *brahmins* who are considered a priestly class, eat fish and fish is considered vegetarian food. There is no Bengali house which doesn't have a small pond in front of their house where they grow fish. They eat fresh fish! Enlightened master Ramakrishna Paramahamsa used to eat fish regularly. For Bengalis, fish, sweet and tobacco are the basic requirements. Coming to the immoral habit of smoking, Ramakrishna used to smoke! Vivekananda used to smoke! They were enlightened masters, without a doubt. Of course, they smoked not as addiction but as a technique to keep themselves in their body. Enlightened masters develop some habit that would keep them in the body on planet Earth, or else their pull in the upward direction simply causes them to leave the body.

So what is this so called 'morality' about? It is just local customs and traditions. In the course of time, they become moral principles. If you read the ancient scriptures, the great epics of India such as the *Mahabharata*, you will see that Princess Draupadi was married to five men! She lived with five men! If that was the case today, she would be in prison! There are so many different kinds of life systems with so many different kinds of customs. In the *Mahabharata*, Kunti had five sons from five different men!

There are so many kinds of morality; so many kinds of life structures and so many kinds of thinking systems. At different times, different rules were formed by different leaders. In some societies, something is considered moral, while in some other society, the same thing is considered immoral. In some society, something is right and in some other society, the same thing is wrong.

Here in America, in a particular state, casinos are allowed, while in the neighboring state, casinos are illegal. A river separates the two states and in the border line on the river between the two states there is a big casino! On one side it is legal, and on the other side it is illegal! Something can be a law in one place and the same thing can be illegal in an adjoining place.

So how does one scale right and wrong? Where is the scale to measure what is right and what is wrong? There is no scale. That is why in *Sanatana Dharma*, which is the correct name for Hinduism, we have two scriptures. *Sanatana Dharma* is the only courageous *dharma* (system of righteousness), to have two kinds of scriptures. In all other religions on planet Earth, they have only one scripture, only one ultimate holy book. And in most of the religions their holy book cannot be updated.

Sanatana Dharma is the only courageous religion which says its holy books can be updated. The scriptures here have been divided into two portions: *Sruti* (*Vedas* and *Upanishads*) and *Smriti* (epics, books of conduct, etc). *Sruti* consists of the ultimate laws about enlightenment; *Atman* (the Self); *Brahman* (the divinity); the concept of self realization, of the universe and so on. *Smriti* consists of the social laws, day-to-day rules and regulations.

Hindus are the first courageous people who declared that their *Smriti* can be changed. From time to time, enlightened masters could create new *Smriti* because it is known that no moral principles can be moral principles forever. No law can be a law forever because both morality and law are based on situations, based on the type of people involved. If the deer population becomes too much, we are allowed to hunt. Similarly at one time, the population of cows was excessive in India. This resulted in cows being given away in sacrifices. Once the number of cows became low, they started to worship cows again. It is all done with supreme awareness and in smooth harmony with nature.

These rules are created to maintain equilibrium in society; to maintain harmony in society. When we all live together, we need to understand and follow a few basic principles to live happily. For instance, you will not try to kill me so that I will not kill you. We both can live happily without fear. Like this, a few basic principles are drawn and put into being. Slowly they become rules. Then they become moral principles.

As long as we understand the root of these moral principles, we will neither behave immorally nor will we be disturbed by these moral codes. The problem arises when we are not taught the basis of these rules. When we don't know the basis, they become forced rules. Then, we not only try to step around these rules, but we also create deep guilt within ourselves when we disobey them. We get caught in this cycle of guilt because of a sheer lack of understanding.

When anything is a forced rule, we always try to break it. For instance, we always speed when we don't see the policeman around. Actually, there is some sense of adventure and satisfaction when doing things that one is not supposed to do.

A man who became addicted to smoking came to me asking for help, 'Master, please help me to quit smoking. I don't know how I became addicted. Please help me.'
I asked him, 'How did you start?'
He replied, 'Master, I never wanted to smoke. In fact, I hated the smell! One day my friend and I were talking on a street corner. My friend was smoking. My father saw us from a distance and thought that I was also smoking. When I went home, he started shouting at me. I tried my best to explain to him that I was not smoking, but he would not listen to me. So I thought, anyhow he is not willing to believe me and he is already shouting at me for smoking, so I might as well smoke! I had already been punished. That is why I started smoking.'

Most of the time, if we are asked not to do something, we feel provoked into doing it. We feel a sort of joy or satisfaction in doing it. That is a basic tendency in every human being. When you say 'no' to your parents, you prove you are a man. As long as you say 'yes', you are only a child. You feel you are not mature until you start saying 'no'. When you say 'no', you feel mature! It is a basic tendency.

You can see this in teenagers, especially in the Western countries. The moment they say 'no', they think they are grown-up and mature. They feel they have become mature, that they have become a man or woman by saying 'no' to their parents. That is why there are so many rebellious groups; so many so-called 'gangs'. It is because there is a deep satisfaction in saying 'no'.

Saying 'no' is addictive. When we say 'no', we are trying to prove we are somebody special - that we are a distinct individual. As long as moral principles are forced on us without any understanding of their source, we create two things; first, the desire to move away from them, and second, deep guilt within our being.

Two children were talking about their grandparents. One child said to the other, 'My grandmother talks a lot. I can't understand how she can talk so much. What does your grandma do?'
The other child replied, 'My Grandma crams in as many pages of the Bible as she can from morning till night.'
The first child asked, 'How come? Why does she do it?' The other friend replied, 'She says she is preparing for her final exam.'

The way in which morality and religion are projected to us, we pray only out of fear and guilt; that is the problem.

Another small story:

A great pundit - learned man - wanted to bathe in the sacred river, Ganges. He had a kamandalu (water pot) with him. He needed to keep it safe while he bathed. He looked around, but there seemed to be nobody trustworthy around who would keep it while he had his bath in river. So he made a small pit in the sand on the banks of the river, placed his kamandalu in it and covered the pit with sand. In order to remember where he had buried the kamandalu, he put a heap of sand on that spot. He then went to bathe in the river.
There was a farmer watching the pundit from a distance. He saw what the pundit had done. He thought to himself, 'Oh! I did not know that one is supposed to make a small sand mound on the river bank before bathing in the Ganges!' He immediately made a heap of sand similar to that of the pundit and then entered the Ganges to bathe.
Another person came to the river bank just then and saw the farmer making a small sand mound. He thought, 'Oh! It seems to be a tradition to make a sand mound before bathing in the Ganges.' He too made a small sand mound and went in to bathe.

By and by, all the people who came to the river for their bath started making sand mounds before entering the Ganges.
When the pundit returned from his bath in the river, he saw hundreds of sand mounds all over the river bank! He was now in trouble. Where was his kamandalu? Under which heap of sand was it hidden? He started to search, destroying the sand mounds.
Suddenly the freshly bathed farmer returned and shouted at him saying, 'Why are you destroying our Shivalingas? (symbol of God Shiva) Why are you destroying our sand mounds? You are a pundit, you should have some sense! Don't you know that one is supposed to make a Shivalinga before bathing in the Ganges? You are destroying our Shivalingas. Don't you have any sense?'
A sand mound naturally looks like a Shivalinga. The pundit wondered, 'What is this man talking about? When did this ritual start? It was me who just kept my kamandalu in a sand pit and now it has become a Shivalinga with a big following! I don't think I can do anything about this now.' He was not allowed to destroy the sand mounds. He had to move on without his kamandalu.

If we look into our lives, there are so many mounds that have entered it in the same way. There are so many speed breakers; so many obstacles that have entered our lives without any solid basis. By and by, with the passage of time, many regulations which were meaningful in the past have become rules in the present without having any meaning!

In India, in the olden days, they would not do any sewing work after sunset. As they used needles to sew at night in the dim light of a hurricane lamp, it was difficult to sew and so it was customary not to sew after sunset. Even now in India, we can see that after sunset, people will not do any sewing! Not even in some of the tailor shops where there are bright tube lights! There are so many tailor shops that have electrical lights, but they will not sew by hand after sunset. They may use machines, but never the hand alone.

When we don't have the correct understanding, practices become dead rules. When we have the correct understanding, any rule can become a technique to live life happily. When we have understanding, we will realize that rules facilitate happy, blissful lives for ourselves and people around us. We will automatically fall in line with them. Otherwise these very rules create hell for us and others.

I have seen a few people who sit down for meditation. Before they start their meditation, they create such a fuss at home! They will shout, 'Keep quiet, don't shout, switch off the music, do this, do that.' They practically turn the whole house upside down for the sake of ten minutes of meditation. Do you think that they will even manage ten minutes of meditation? The moment they start, they are either distracted, or dozing, or killing the mosquitoes sitting on them, or scratching some body part. At the end of it, they think they have done enough for the day. For this minor effort at meditation, they create so much drama! They practically turn the whole house upside down without understanding that meditation itself is done for the sake of peace in the house! Their meditation becomes a torture for the others at home!

Some people, when they try to silence others create a big noise themselves. They will be telling others to keep quiet in such a loud voice! In schools sometimes, one can see teachers make more noise than the children in trying to keep them quiet!

Anyhow, most of the time when we don't understand the root of moral principles, we start living in a dull and dead manner. According to me, any rule if internalized, will create guilt in us. Understand: it could be any rule. When I say 'any', I mean 'any rule'. Any rule which we follow without experiencing its essence will create a deep guilt in us because by nature we aspire for freedom. *Svabhava swatantrata* means our nature itself is freedom. We are free by our very nature. We are *nithya muktas* - eternally free. We never want to be caged! We never want to be slaves to rules!

Actually, if you see, society is struggling - working only towards attaining freedom. Our entire struggle is nothing but a struggle for freedom. Even our search for money is the search for freedom. If we have more money, we have bigger choices, bigger house, bigger car, more comforts; more freedom. Our choice for freedom is the real search. Our search for money is nothing but a search for freedom. So by our very nature we are searching for freedom. We never wanted to be caught by rules or moral principles. When some moral principle is given to us as a rule, either we try to go beyond it or if we can't, we take revenge on the people who imposed the rule on us. We always take revenge. We wait for the right time and take revenge on them.

People come and tell me, 'Master, my son is not taking care of me.' Be very clear: your son may be your worst enemy and you may be his worst enemy because you have imposed so many rules, so many regulations on him. You have laid down so many laws; you were his guide when he was young. Naturally, one part of his mind will respect you, while the other part will always be against you. The other part will be waiting to take revenge on you because you imposed rules and regulations on him. Therefore it can be expected that he will naturally be against you. This may not be obvious but it will be true at the subconscious level.

There are a few people who try to give us rules in a very subtle or cunning manner. They exploit our fear and greed by showing us hell and heaven; desire for heaven and fear of hell. They create so many concepts of hell and heaven in us. They say, 'If you practice a certain way of life, you will be rewarded with heaven; if you practice other ways of life, you will be rewarded with hell.' This concept of heaven and hell is a subtle way of exploiting our being.

When we are given rules based on greed and fear, it leads to the creation of deep guilt in us. This is one of the ultimate laws which is very difficult to understand. Nobody can live their life based on any law. When I say nobody, I mean nobody. When I say any law, I mean any law. Life is far superior to laws. All laws, rules and regulations are based on some understanding of life. But life is beyond our understanding and beyond our logic. People ask me, 'Why is life created at all?' I tell them, this 'why' can never be answered because this 'why' is based on your logic.

Life is based on God's logic. Our logic and God's logic can never meet. His logic is so big, so vast and so infinite. We can never meet His logic. Life is created by Him. Rules are created by us. Life is created by Him. Laws are created by us. Naturally, our laws can never match or fit with God's logic or God-created life. Life is natural. Laws are societal. Life is physical. Laws are mental. So all our ideas, all our do's and don'ts, all our morality, all our right or wrong is given to us by society.

We are called a saint or a sinner only by society. As long as we are given the title 'saint' by society, we are saints. The moment society gives us the title 'sinner', we are sinners. If we kill someone in society, we will be called murderers. We will be punished. If we kill someone in war, we will be called heroes. We will be rewarded with a big award! So understand that these things are purely societal. When we start internalizing the laws of society in our minds, we create a deep wound in our beings; we destroy our intelligence. According to me, rules and regulations are only superficial. All our concepts of morality are shallow; just look a little deeper! They are only skin deep!

In some religions, people are made to believe that they are born sinners. They live their entire life in guilt. This situation offers the religious leaders control over people through the fear element. The only sin, the 'original sin', is the ignorance of not realizing the truth – that we too are divine; that divinity is eternally present in us; that our true nature is to be blissful. When we believe that we are sinners, we commit the biggest sin. Once we throw away this guilt, the guilt that comes from the belief that we are born sinners until somebody saves us, we become liberated, and realize that we are already one with the divine.

Our true nature is always struggling to express itself, to go beyond all rules, regulations and all moral principles. Our consciousness is always trying to break through our conscience. Our consciousness continuously fights with our conscience. Conscience is societal. Consciousness is natural. Conscience is a poor substitute for consciousness.

People ask me, 'What is this, master? You are breaking basic laws. You are pulling down the whole social structure. You are pulling down the whole structure of rules and regulations. Then how can we all live morally? How will people live without morality? Why are you doing this?'

You see: for children, we need rules to introduce them to morality. But for us, it is time! We are not children anymore! It is time to stand up and have morals based on understanding, not based on fear and greed. As long as morality is based on fear and greed, you can be sure that it is just skin deep. You can never be moral based on fear and greed. If fear and greed are the basis for your moral values, you will try all possible ways to escape them. For instance, you will speed just ten miles over the local speed limit and think, 'As soon as I see a policeman, I can press the brake and slow down.'

As long as your moral values are based on fear and greed, understand that you are still a child. You are not a mature adult. If you are really grown up, your moral principles will be based on understanding, not on fear and greed. According to me, a mature person means a person who lives a happy, blissful and quiet life without fear and greed. When we drop our fear and greed, a new kind of morality arises in our being; a morality which is different from social morality; a morality that is not superficial. It arises out of our being. Our entire being experiences a different kind of well-being.

Let me tell you a beautiful story:

There was a Zen master in a small village. For some unknown reason, the King of the land declared that this master should be killed the next morning. The Zen master was informed of the king's orders. The King had also said that the Zen master could do whatever he wanted until the next morning. He could live as he liked; he was given complete freedom.

But the master was seen following his daily routine even on his last day. He was seen gardening, fetching water from the well, cooking, serving his disciples and living in the same manner as before, like it was just another routine day.

His disciples asked him, 'You are about to die tomorrow morning. Don't you want to do something else?' The master replied, 'My life is based on a clear understanding. This is the best way I can live. I am totally fulfilled. I have nothing else I desire to do, whether I live for 24 hours or 2 hours. This is what I want to do. This is my enjoyment.'

If somebody gives us a similar deadline, 'You will only live till tomorrow morning; you can do whatever you want until then,' just look inside your mind; think of all the things you would do! You would probably live a life on this last day that you would never have lived before because of your suppression in the name of morality. That is why I say: our morality is superficial. We are controlling ourselves for some reason that we are not fully convinced about. We are not living life. As long as we don't live life, we will always feel that we are missing something. The feeling that we are missing something is the primary reason why we fear death. Mostly, we are not afraid of death itself. We are afraid that we have not lived our life fully and therefore we are afraid to die! Actually, it is not fear of death. It is the fear of not having lived life fully.

Guilt is the root of fear of death. This is an important thing we should understand! Guilt is the root of greed also! As long as we suffer from guilt, we can never enjoy anything. One of my devotees told me, 'Master, the moment I see an ice-cream, I get a cold. I don't even have to eat it. If I just look at an ice-cream, I catch a cold.' She had been suffering for the last twelve years. I attempted to trace the root of the problem with her; it was almost like psychoanalysis. I traced it to its root cause. Her mother created guilt in her about eating an ice-cream when she was a child. The mother didn't want her to eat too much ice-cream, so she created guilt in her; a deep negative attitude towards ice-cream. The negative attitude was responsible for the allergic reaction triggered just by looking at ice-cream. When we were talking, she said, 'Sometimes when I see an ice-cream, I can hear my mother's voice saying, 'Don't eat!' Even now I can hear her voice.'

All of us hear voices in us. Actually, we don't even know how many times we hear voices! We are not so sensitive, which is why we don't realize we can hear voices. Our being is a crowd of voices. Understand: we have reached a stage where our being is not just our being; it is a totality of a crowd of voices. All the voices are there: our mother's voice, father's voice, teacher's voice, neighbor's voice, professor's voice, our hero's voice, etc. We are a sum total of a crowd of voices. That is why we feel there is so much contradiction inside ourselves. If there were only one voice, we would never have a problem; our mind would flow like a river.

This is a beautiful analogy that we should understand. The mind is like a river; like a stream! Guilt is like the rocks in the river. It blocks the flow, creating whirlpools, creating energy blocks. Any guilt we carry in our being is blocking energy. Similar to a blood clot, this is an energy clot. All the voices which are inside our mind are the cause of guilt. And this guilt kills our intelligence.

As long as we flow like a river, like a stream, we will express extraordinary intelligence in our lives. We will express a different kind of intelligence; a different kind of energy; a different kind of bliss.

The moment we start creating guilt in ourselves, the moment we are stopped in our free flow, we create an energy clot inside our being; we create an energy clot in our mind. The older the culture, the greater the guilt. We tend to think that if our culture is old, we are better in some manner and so more guilt happens when we do things. All this will get offset when you operate out of consciousness.

Also, the older the culture, the lesser the understanding of it, because over generations, it gets diluted in understanding. If we live based on past rules without comprehending why these rules were created, we will create a deep wound inside our beings. We will create a deep wound inside our minds.

After talking to this lady, I came to the conclusion that it was her mother's voice that was creating the disturbance. I gave her a simple technique. I told her, 'Just get yourself five ice-creams; don't bother about your mother. If you hear your mother's voice, just be angry with her and eat the ice-cream.'

Anger is a beautiful way to release guilt. The moment we express anger, guilt is also released. Actually, anger and guilt are two sides of the same coin. Anger is a wonderful way to release guilt. The moment we become angry with the person who is responsible for creating guilt in us, we release the guilt.

When we create guilt within ourselves based on somebody's opinion, how do we create that guilt? We create it because we respect that person. The moment we become angry with him, naturally that respect is lost. We understand we have been exploited and are disturbed by it. Quite often that person may not even realize he was exploiting us.

A small incident happened a few months back.

An American lady brought her son to me with a complaint. She said, 'Master, he is not obeying me. Please advise him.'
I felt a little awkward. I never obeyed my mother. How could I advise this boy to obey his mother? The boy looked intelligent. But the mother kept pestering me, so I had no other option.
I started talking to the boy. I asked him, 'Why don't you obey your mother? She made even me obey her just now. Why don't you listen

to what she is saying?'
The boy looked at me and replied, 'Master, she herself is not happy. If I follow her words, where will I end up? I will also end up in the same way. Why are you asking me to obey her? Why are you asking me to listen to her?'

I was shocked! Somehow I managed to convince him for the sake of his mother. But I think the next generation is going to sue their parents if they fall into depression! Children are going to sue the parents. They will say, 'My parents didn't give me the correct mental set-up which is why I am now depressed.' Be careful! We have to find a means by which we will not create guilt in the minds of children; a method by which we will create only more intelligence, more understanding and more bliss in their lives.

According to me, experience is more solid than morality. Consciousness is more solid than conscience. Of course, we need a little patience to create consciousness. We need to work on children; we need to explain every step to them; we can't just spoon-feed them. We can't just spoon-feed consciousness. We can spoon-feed conscience; just do's and don'ts. But with consciousness, we can't do that. We need to work with children. Unless we have this much patience, we have no right to bring one more life to this planet. People come and tell me, 'Master, you don't know, it is very difficult. If you had a child you would understand. You say these things, but it is very difficult to manage them or kindle their intelligence. We have to create guilt and give them rules.'

If you can't take the responsibility, you must think twice before you decide to give birth to a child. Understand! Have you solved your life's problems? Have you found solutions to all your problems? Then go ahead; bring the next generation to this planet. Otherwise... wait! There is every chance the next generation will demand of you, 'What are you doing? Why did you bring me into this world?' Already children have begun to ask, 'She herself is not happy. Why should I follow her?'

There is every chance that tomorrow's children are not going to listen to our idea of morality.

Not only for the sake of our children but for our own sake we should look into our lives. I think that Vivekananda was one of the most courageous masters who lived on this planet. He had nothing to do with the so-called society. He broke every rule; he gave a new light to humanity. I believe He was *Manu* - The sage who coded a book on social laws - of modern days. He was the *smriti kara* - creator of social laws - of modern days.

He said in one of his discourses, 'Reason and Religion': let religion be flooded with logic. Let your religion be flooded either by reason or by logic. Let whatever that can be washed away by reasoning, be washed away. The earlier they are washed away, the better it is for humanity.'

He said, 'flood religion with reasoning.' Allow reason to be the main thing. Let our consciousness be the torch, while we flood religion. The earlier the superstitions are washed away, the better it is for humanity. If they can't stand the flood of reason or logic, let them be washed away. It is better for humanity.

A small story:

There was a scientist, Galileo, who discovered that the Earth was not flat, that it was in fact a globe. He wrote after his research that the planet Earth was round; it was a globe; it was not flat. But the Christian Inquisition at that time, was so convinced that they were the total authority, and the 'church' had such complete control over the culture, that they succeeded in forcing Galileo to recant his discovery of fact. In their ignorance, they knew the Sun went around the Earth, and were not going to be told otherwise by a scientist.

So the Christian court, the Inquisitors, summoned the scientist. They called him and said, 'You can't say that our planet Earth moves around the Sun. You have to change your statement, otherwise you will be killed.' In those days, they were not only killing anyone who disagreed with them, they were also torturing in very un-Christian ways. Galileo finally agreed saying, 'Alright, I will change my statement.' He changed his statement to this: 'My earlier statement was wrong. The Sun moves around the Earth.' He made a small footnote in this book:

Because I am Christian, I have changed my statement. But the Sun and planet Earth are not Christians. So they go around as they go around. They are not going to change their direction of movement based on my statement.

When someone points to the moon with their hand, if you grab their hand, naturally you miss looking at the moon because you have changed the direction of their hand. The next generation ends up looking somewhere else. Not only do we miss looking at the moon, we ensure that the next generation also misses looking at the moon. As long as there is understanding, there is nectar in our lives. It creates tremendous intelligence in our life. The moment understanding is reduced to a superstitious belief, the moment it is reduced to morality, it creates deep guilt in us. And guilt is the sure killer of intelligence. It will not allow us move on in our lives.

I would like to tell you about an incident. A devotee had a tumor at the end of her spinal cord near the root *chakra*. She had suffered for twenty years. She came to me and said, 'Master, please help me, heal me. I have been suffering with this tumor for so many years.' She told me that even after surgery, the tumor came back. I started by talking to her to help trace the origin of the problem.

Finally, she opened up and started to weep. I asked her if she had any guilt related to her sex energy. She told me that she had been abused when she was very young, while she was a child. One of her close relatives had abused her for many years. That guilt stayed with her and she said, 'I started hating that part of my body. I started wishing that that part of my body did not exist. I felt as if that part did not belong to my body. My hatred towards that person was redirected towards my own body.'

Her hatred had become very deep. She slowly opened up to me. When she brought the guilt up, I continued talking to her, helping her come out of the guilt. She was psychologically healed. I explained to her how this was a common occurrence. Studies reveal that one in four children is sexually abused, especially in America. Of course, children don't open up; they don't tell us.

This lady was psychologically healed after I explained the nature of such matters. You will be surprised to hear this, but the lady was cured in just 10 days. The tumor simply disappeared! I had given her a small meditation technique. I told her to meditate on that area while expressing her anger towards the person who abused her. I told her to weep, shout, cry, even hit the person in her visualization; to close the doors of her room, take a pillow, imagine that pillow to be the person, weep, cry, shout and hit the pillow! After that, sit silently and feel that the particular body part was an integral part of her body. You will be surprised: in just 10 days the tumor disappeared. It never came back. It may be difficult to understand, but it is true.

Similar things happen in our lives due to psychological factors. When we fall ill, it is not always a condition of physical ill health. Sometimes we are psychologically disturbed. Most of the time, our energy gets blocked because of guilt. We suffer psychological illness because of our guilt. If we look deep, wherever we have fear, wherever we are unable to move, wherever we are unable to make decisions, there will be some guilt. And because of this, we fall ill.

There are three types of guilt: first, guilt created by immediate family; second, guilt created by social laws; third, guilt created by one's own self. These are the three major kinds of guilt which kill our intelligence. Guilt about sex is generally the guilt created by our immediate family. This is the first guilt. Guilt associated with greed is also created by one's immediate family. Guilt based on fear is created by social laws. The third guilt, which is the worst, is the one which we create ourselves. When we internalize guilt based on greed and fear, we create new types of guilt for ourselves. If we analyze situations in which we find ourselves stuck, or with which we may be struggling, we will find the three kinds of guilt present at the root of the problem.

We must break free from the past. The past is dead. Not only is it dead, it is a dead weight on our being. As long as we have guilt, we will never be able to move forward in our lives blissfully; we can never have deeply blissful lives. Be very clear: we can never be moral based on guilt. If our behavior is based on guilt, our morality becomes immature and superficial. It is time to be mature. We will not behave immorally if we understand that rules are created for our own sake. For instance, if we come to know that there is no punishment in this country for committing murders, will we kill the next person? If one wants to do such a thing, then it means that the person is immature, not grown up. Then such a life is not worth living. He is like the living dead.

For nine years prior to enlightenment, I walked the length and breadth of India; from Tapovan in the north to Kanya Kumari in the south; Ahmedabad in the west to Ganga Sagar in the east. I have walked the length and breadth of India. I have always meditated in graveyards because it was much easier; I didn't ever have to make reservations! People always asked me, 'Weren't you afraid? Did you encounter any ghosts?' I tell them, 'Dead people don't disturb others. Only living people disturb others!' If one's moral principles are based on greed and fear, then be clear that such a life is much worse than being dead. It is not worth living.

Let our morality be based on our understanding, on consciousness, not on conscience. As long as our principles are based on 'do's and don'ts', we are just children. These rules, based on our lack of understanding, form a block between enlightenment and us. As long as these blocks exist we can never touch enlightenment. The moment these blocks are removed, we experience total freedom, total bliss, total ecstasy; then naturally enlightenment happens; we won't have to reach out to enlightenment; enlightenment will reach out to us. Understand that guilt is the sure killer of intelligence. May we kill the guilt and experience the ultimate intelligence!

Our *Upanishads* say, *'prajnanam brahma'* (Intelligence is Existence). May you experience that Existence and experience the Eternal Bliss ... *nithyananda*!

We will spend a few minutes addressing questions. I will now try to answer your questions.

Master, you said that it was unnecessary for someone to do extensive periods of tapas (penance) in their search for enlightenment. How is that possible for a practical man?

What I spoke of is for the practical man. Understand: when I recommend one should do *tapasya* (penance), people say it is impractical. When I say there is no need to do *tapasya*, people ask me to explain in a practical manner why it is not needed. The very understanding can lead you to express enlightenment. The right listening and understanding can lead one to express their innate nature - which is enlightenment!

According to me, enlightenment means being in eternal bliss. When you are in bliss, nothing in the outer world can disturb you. Your outer world will never enter your inner world. That is what I call enlightenment. Simply understand that your outer world is your outer world. Your inner world is your inner world. Whatever you do in the outer world, do it like housekeeping in a dream. What will happen to all our housekeeping done in a dream when we wake up? It simply disappears! That's all! But when you are in the dream, it is intense. If you can maintain this understanding, not only will you do things intensely, you will also not have any attachment to it! That is the way!

Now you may possibly have a few more questions like, 'How does one lead life practically?'

When I refer to housekeeping in a dream, I don't mean, 'Don't do this housekeeping.' Do it, but do it in a way that you are not disturbed by the housekeeping; do it with the simple understanding that our entire life is nothing but housekeeping in a dream! Continue to do the same housekeeping with this clear understanding. It will be more than enough to express enlightenment. You don't need to work to suppress your greed or fear or any other quality. You need to work only on this single idea: that your entire life is housekeeping in a dream! You will then automatically be free from greed and fear and other emotions.

You should feel that, 'I am doing my housekeeping because I enjoy it.' When we were young, we played with toys. When we came to be around 10 years old, we threw away the same toys; we outgrew those toys. Just because we threw away our toys when we were young, it doesn't mean that we will not give toys to our children. Would we say to them, 'I always played with toys when I was young and then threw them away. So don't play with toys?' No! We don't say that. We allow them to play.

We feel a child should play with toys as long as it wants to, till the child reaches maturity. When it becomes mature, it drops the toys automatically. In the same way, we must understand and accept about ourselves, 'Let me play housekeeping in dreams until I really understand.' This very acceptance will lead you to enlightenment. If you are unable to accept, just accept that you are unable to accept it, that is enough! You are pulled towards the past or future only because you don't understand what *is*!

Recently, one of my close devotees asked me, 'Master, you are so casual; so innocent; so playful. But how is it possible that any word you utter becomes true. How can so much intelligence and intuition happen in you continuously? How can you be so playful and paramount at the same time? Your words are clearly turning into reality!'

We should understand something clearly: we are unable to experience intuition because we are unable to fall into the present moment. We are always pulled by either the past or the future. Either we work and worry about the past or we work and worry about the future. Something or the other is continuously going on. And so we miss the present.

Time is like a shaft. Visualize this one thing and understand: time is like a shaft. We are either pulled to this side of the shaft or to that side of the shaft. We never feel relaxed; a deep craving exists within us at all times, either to achieve something in the outer world or to achieve something in the inner world. The craving to achieve something in the inner world is also a craving for the future. Our craving for enlightenment is also worry about the future. Because of craving o some sort, we never fall into the present moment. Remember: eternity penetrates only the present moment.

The first thing to do is to accept the existence of the outer world; accept the existence of the inner world; whatever problems you have in the outer world and whatever problems you have in the inner world, accept them all. As long as you don't accept them, there is a problem.

Just try this small experiment: relax completely for just three days; not more than that; just three days. If you live a satisfied life for just three days, will you lose all your wealth in your inner world or outer world? Surely not! In three days you are not going to lose anything. Why don't you give it a try? For just three days, sincerely, utterly, one hundred percent, drop, accept. If you are unable to accept a hundred percent, accept that you are unable to accept a hundred percent.

Even the acceptance that one is unable to accept themselves in the inner world and outer world will make one drop from the rut of being pulled between past and future. The moment we understand, 'I am not able to accept my reality; there is nothing I can do!' even the very push and pull will become our reality. If we accept everything then we will fall into the present moment. The moment we fall into the present moment, the time shaft will become our servant. As long as we are below the time shaft, it rules us; we will be pulled or pushed by the time shaft. The moment our consciousness is raised to the present moment, we see that we are penetrating the time shaft. When we penetrate the time shaft, the future and the past are clearly known to us. We then come to the tremendous realization that the time shaft exists only due to the projection of our mind!

Try this experiment for just three days; if you can fall into the present moment, relaxing the headaches related to the outer world and the inner world, in three days time, you will have a glimpse.

What is life? What does it mean 'to live in the present moment'? You will experience such ecstasy, such a different space, such a different life when you live in the present moment. Three days! You must attempt to not alter anybody in the outer world after this experience. After all you have lived based on your own changing philosophies for the last 30 years. Give yourself just three days for a trial. You will see when you experiment with these great techniques, how they work miracles in your being, how they start working alchemy in your being.

A sincere three days trial; if you are unable to be sincere, accept that you are not able to be sincere. Even that sincerity is enough. You will start seeing a different space in you. That different space is what I call *nithya* - eternity.

May you experience that *nithya* - eternity and *nithyananda* - eternal bliss!

Love To Survive

Many of us think that love is a choice. We feel that the experience of love and expression of love are choices that we can make. If we want, we can have it. If we don't want, we can leave it. But it is not so. As a human being, it is as basic a necessity as it is to be alive.

Can we think of experiencing love and then expressing it to be a choice? No! It is not a choice as we think. When we experience love, there is no choice but to express it. If we don't experience and express love, we may inhale and exhale, but we can't say we are alive. There are so many animals which are breathing in and breathing out, so many other lives which are there on this planet. In a sense one can't say all of them are living; even to feel that one is living, love is a basic necessity.

Let us look a little deeper into the meaning of the word love. The word love is too contaminated and too loaded with many different meanings, interpretations, commentaries. Forget the idea of selfless, unconditional, spiritual love. We don't even need to bother about that yet. Let us first consider normal, simple love with all its possessiveness, jealousy and whatever other side effects it may cause! Even that love does a lot for our body and mind. After that we can look at selfless and spiritual love or mature love.

First, let us analyze love, the feeling of affection that we share in our normal day-to-day lives, which has so many side effects and after effects like possessiveness, jealousy and anger. All these are the after effects of ordinary love. Even this love does a lot for our bodies, does a lot of good for our minds.

I was reading a magazine the other day which contained a survey report. I was amazed to see the report. The title was, *Live Forever*. It gave eleven techniques, eleven important instructions to extend one's life by at least 20 years, supported by standard statistics and survey reports. All the eleven were related to love. It said that even caring for a pet animal releases a hormone which allows you to live at ease with your body. If caring for your pet animal does so much, surely caring for your husband or for your wife will do a lot more!

Another point it stated was about how people die early if they are single or are widowers, and how life gets extended if we are caring for, or being cared for by somebody. Also, in the second case, it is said that there are lower chances of cancer and depression. Even what we call ordinary love, simple infatuation, can do miracles for our body and mind. It gives a deep feeling of healing, of well being. I am not advocating infatuation. I am trying to explain what even ordinary love can do to a person. Ultimately, all infatuation should end in pure love.

A small analysis from *Tantra*, a part of Hindu philosophy: *Tantra* says that there are five types of restlessness that we all suffer from which can be healed by ordinary love - ordinary, simple, human love - the feeling of caring for each other; I am not speaking of high spiritual love, what we call *bhakti* or devotion, selfless love – which is seeing the whole world as God - this comes later.

Let us first talk of simple practical love which we may share for some reason; either because that person supports us socially or that person will stand up for us when we face difficult times, or because we feel that the person supports us mentally or psychologically, or maybe we want a good certificate or name from him. For any of these reasons, we may show love. Even love expressed with a selfish reason heals us from five different kinds of restlessness.

The first kind of restlessness happens due to the place. Sometimes in a particular place or situation we feel restless. If we move from that place or situation, we feel more settled. Even in such places or such situations, an expression of love - even the body language of love can make things better; it can heal.

Becoming comfortable with the space around us makes us less tense, less restless. A house becomes a home when we live in it with love and care. Similarly, any place can become home to us if we choose to love and care for it. We should find simple things that we like about a new location, things that we can relate to and things that can make us smile. Once this is done, the rest is simple; love will break through the rest.

The next type of restlessness is due to physical reasons. Physical restlessness is a form of tension within our body. Any tension in our bodies, any uneasiness can be released when we express our love to somebody. You may ask: how love can take away physical restlessness. We can see in our own lives - a mother who has a child to look after, feels continuously rejuvenated; otherwise taking care of children is not an easy job! She feels rejuvenated because of the love and care she feels for the child.

Tension or restlessness in our body is removed when we care for somebody, when we smile at somebody, when we express love in our body language. In fact, you can try it out. At the time you feel tense inside your body, just decide consciously and melt with love towards somebody. That very moment, the tension will disappear! For example, you may be lying down feeling unwell. If some friend visits you at that time or when somebody you love visits, you immediately sit up and talk to them and feel better, is it not? You feel instantly rejuvenated. When you really love somebody, you express your energy. Even a simple smile can cause this switch this to happen if that smile comes from our heart. This is why they say, 'When you meet someone without a smile, give them yours!'

There are four things we need to understand: love, intelligence, energy and bliss. All these four feelings are four sides of the same pillar. When we express a feeling through our head, it is intelligence. When we express through our heart, it is love. When we express through our being, it is energy. When our being just relaxes without any reason, it is bliss! All the four are the same phenomena, expressed through four different names.

So whenever we express love, we express energy also. Love is concentrated and caring energy. So naturally, whenever we express love, we become a channel for energy, and when we are a channel for energy, we not only help others, but are also helped ourselves.

Any mental restlessness can be healed by love. When we care for pets or play with children, we can avoid heart attacks; these can postpone any fatal disease. Pets release tension. They do not talk back to us. They just listen and express love. Their energy heals us.

The next type of restlessness is the restlessness of emotion. Mental restlessness is different; that is intellectual. Emotional restlessness means the restlessness which cannot be controlled by a few words, just by consoling oneself. It can be healed only when we express love. When we start radiating love, it floods our being with energy. Our being is opened to the higher energies. This heals our emotional restlessness.

Ultimately we come to spiritual restlessness. Just the pure love for your teacher or master can heal spiritual restlessness! Many people come and tell me, 'Master, just by being in your presence we are able to meditate. Why are we not able to meditate at home?' The reason is, whenever we meet great people - swamis and saints - we start relating with them, we start expressing our love towards them. This heals our spiritual restlessness completely. What do I mean by 'spiritual restlessness'? It is the inability to sit comfortably with oneself, alone, in silence.

I see so many people; they can sit with others, with the television, with the newspaper; but they can't sit with themselves! This is what I call spiritual restlessness. They know to spend time with everybody but they do not know how to spend time with themselves.

If you observe me as I speak, you will notice long gaps between successive words. In those gaps, my intention is to bring down the feeling of spiritual restlessness in you. People who are not spiritually inclined, who are not mature enough to listen to these great ideas, can never sit and listen to spiritual discourses, at least with me. This is because their mind continuously needs food; it is constantly jumping from thought to thought. When I create gaps of silence in my talks, immediately boredom shows up in these people! Their mind will say, 'I must leave. There is nothing happening here.' Only a man who can sit with himself can listen to these great words. If he can't even sit with himself, how can he be helped even if he listens to my words?

The mind is such that it continuously demands information; it waits impatiently for the next word. Why are we so comfortable in front of the television or in a cinema theater? There is so much material being pushed inside our being without a gap, that's why. So much information, so many ideas are sent inside our being to support our restlessness. So we feel very comfortable. Why do we enjoy food that is spicy? Again, too much is sent inside, that's why. When you feel like scratching an itch, you feel comfortable because again when you scratch, you get busy! Spicy food is nothing but 'scratching' the tongue. It is a sort of comfort when information is flooding our mind.

There is one thing you should understand about watching movies. When you are traveling at 30 km per hour, you can read all the signboards; see all the trees and the scenery around clearly. If you are moving at a speed of 130 km per hour, will we be able to see anything clearly? There are far too many frames per second for our senses to grasp anything. If the number of frames is less than 6 per second, you can clearly read and understand the information on display. If the number of frames is more than 6 per second, your consciousness cannot relate through the eyes anymore. While watching a movie or television, you are exposed to 12 to 16 frames per second. So naturally your consciousness is just pushed aside! And because we are disconnected from our consciousness, we simply fall for the scene that we see. If the hero of the movie dies, although we may be well aware of the fact that the actor is alive and making his next movie, we cry for his death! We are educated, logical and intellectual people; we are aware that what we are viewing is just a movie, but still, we laugh with the scene, cry with the scene and experience changing moods with it.

In this way, scratching, spicy food, movies are all things which keep flooding our systems with information or sensations. This creates a deep restlessness as a side effect. If we have this deep restlessness, we cannot sit and listen to great spiritual ideas; and I make sure that people with restlessness do not sit here because they not only don't understand, but they also misunderstand!

Misunderstanding great truths is very dangerous; a half truth is worse than a lie. So if one has the patience to sit and listen to these words, one's spiritual restlessness comes down; also the probability of our mind demanding constant information in the form of the next thought also comes down. We become so passive that these thoughts not only touch our heads, but directly touch our hearts as well. If we are totally passive, our being opens up at the emotional level. If we are totally relaxed, at ease with ourselves, without too many thoughts crowding our minds, we will see that our being just absorbs these great truths.

In Vedanta we say, *'shravana, manana* and *nididhyasam'* to describe this process of calming down. It is listening, meditating and practicing. If our minds are calm, there is no need to meditate separately. The very listening can create the same experience, can become the experience; *'shravana'* - listening, can lead to experience. According to me, if our *'shravana'* is not proper, even *'manana'* - meditating, cannot help; contemplating silently cannot help.

J.Krishnamurthi says that listening to God - deep, total listening without restlessness, is divine. That itself is God.

If we look deeply into our being, the very presence of a master heals the spiritual restlessness. Love towards the master heals spiritual restlessness.

So our love, even if it is simple and normal love, heals all five aspects of restlessness.

Now let us look into the higher type of love, the love that was experienced by Meera, Chaitanya, Ramakrishna, and Ramana Maharishi, all the great saints. Ramakrishna said, 'My love for the divine is a miser's love for his money, a chaste wife's love for her husband, a mother's love for her child - all these three put together *and something more!'* Of course, we will not be able to understand such love through these definitions. Love for the divine is a feeling of being one with the other; falling in tune with the other person in totality; it is an ecstatic feeling, the highest expression of our being.

Just by the utterance of the word 'Krishna', Meera would experience ecstasy. In the scriptures, it is said, 'If tears roll down as you listen to God's name, be sure that it is your last *janma* (birth)'. Ramakrishna also makes a similar comment in his 'Gospel of Ramakrishna'.

If we listen to the devotional songs sung by Annamacharya on Lord Balaji, we realize that the Divine is an actual experience for him.

In some of his verses, Ramana Maharishi laments before Arunachala, the Lord of Tiruvannamalai. He says, 'You are my house owner, my husband. How then can you stand by and watch while thieves come in and take me away, O Arunachala?' What a beautiful verse! The five senses are referred to as the thieves who come into the house and take away the being that is him; Arunachala is the soul, the divine self within.

Somebody asked Ramana Maharishi, *'Bhagwan,* how can you say these things to God?' *Bhagwan* replied, 'For you, God is just a faith, just a belief; for me He is a living being.'

A small story:

A devotee had been praying to Vishnu for ten years but never got a darshan (vision) of Him. So he decided to stop worshipping Vishnu and pray to Shiva instead. He set Vishnu's statue aside and placed one of Shiva before him and started worshipping it.
One day, he lit incense sticks before the Shiva statue. The incense smoke rose up towards the Vishnu statue. The man became very angry. He had prayed to Vishnu for so many years and never got blessed with a darshan. He reached out and held Vishnu's nose as he did not want Vishnu to enjoy the lit incense sticks.
As he was pressing the nose, suddenly he felt like he was actually pressing a live nose. He opened his eyes to see Vishnu in front of him; Vishnu was giving him a darshan! His hand dropped from the Lord's nose and he exclaimed, 'O Lord! For so many years you did not grant me a darshan and now when I am denying you the perfume of these incense sticks, why do you give me your darshan?'

Vishnu replied, 'When you prayed to me all these years , you did not feel that I was alive in that statue; only now when you put your hand to my nose in anger, did you have the intensity of feeling that I was actually there in the statue. When you have such a deep feeling of connection, I have to come down and give you a *darshan!*'

There are so many very intense incidents, which express the power of love. Love can perform miracles in your being, not only at the mental level, but even at the physical level. Ramakrishna used to say that sometimes after performing *puja* to Mother Kali, he would wonder whether Mother was alive in the idol, or whether he was wasting his time worshipping a stone. So he used to place a small thread in front of the idol's nose to check whether She was breathing or not. He said the thread always moved with the flow of Her breath!

When we express our deep love, we will see that Existence never misses in relating or responding to us! We can give life to the whole of Existence with love. With just this feeling, it is possible to make the whole world come alive. Whatever we see, feel and experience, then becomes a joyful thing.

Through another small incident, we can see what love can do:

There is a story in the life of Sadashiva Brahmendra, one of the great saints of South India. He always went around without any clothing. He lived just like a child.
One day he was walking in deep ecstasy, when the Nawab - the Muslim ruler of that territory - went riding by. The saint was in such deep ecstasy that he did not notice or pay respect to the Nawab. The Nawab turned wild with fury and cut off the saint's hand with his sword.
Sadashiva Brahmendra continued to walk, hardly noticing the absence of his hand. But one of his devotees started weeping, 'O master! You have lost your hand for not showing courtesy to the Nawab.'
The saint was surprised and asked her to bring the severed hand. He then put it back on and it became whole again!
The devotee was dumbstruck when she saw this.
The saint explained, 'The Nawab's hatred destroyed my hand; your love healed it!'

Love has the power to heal.

Ramana Maharishi always used to say, 'It is the love of devotees which keeps me in the body.' Any master comes down and lives in his body just because of the love of his devotees. Masters as such have no *karma* (unfulfilled actions); they have nothing to achieve, nothing to gain. They don't have anything to enjoy. Then why do they remain in the body? Only because of the love of their devotees.

When we express normal love with all its expectations, it heals five different kinds of restlessness. However, love without expectation simply performs miracles! Ordinary love gives us life; selfless love gives life to even the stone that we worship! Even stone can become God, even an ordinary man can become a guru. Such is the power of faith.

A beautiful incident from the great Hindu epic Ramayana:

Rama, the hero of the epic had to go to Lanka with his entire army to bring back his wife Sita. Sita was held in captivation by the villainous Ravana. There is an ocean that he had to cross to reach Lanka. A bridge had to be built across the ocean to accomplish the task.

Rama ordered one of his devotees, Jambavan - the great bear - to take care of the construction of the bridge across the ocean.
He asked his best devotee, Hanuman, to fly across the sea to first locate Sita. Hanuman said, 'Oh Lord, you are asking Jambavan to construct the bridge and asking me to fly to Lanka. How can I do it?'
Rama replied, 'You just chant the name Rama and you will be able to accomplish the mission. Chanting the name of Rama is more powerful than my physical form.'
Hanuman obeyed him without an iota of doubt and accomplished the task!

Love gives rise to faith and gives life even to stone. Selfish love, when expressed, heals your five feelings of restlessness and gives life to you. Selfless love gives life to everything around you. When you express selfless love, it gives more life to other beings as well.

Therefore, love to survive and to give life. Whether the love is selfish or selfless, start expressing love. Let that become your body language. Let that become your lifestyle. Let that become your very life itself. May you feel and experience eternal bliss - *nithyananda*.

Questions and Answers

Master, can you please explain what part divinity plays in a miracle? You say miracles happen. Does divinity make them happen? What are you referring to as divinity?

In any action, normally you understand three things: first, the person who does it, second is the act and the third is the thing that is done; the doer, the deed and the result. All these three things can be understood as three separate things logically, in this normal plane.

In the ultimate plane of reality there are no three different things. You ask what role divinity plays in a miracle. The very miracle itself is divinity. When you ask this question, you are asking for cause, effect and the act; you are asking whether divinity is the cause, the act or the effect. In the language of divinity, these three different things do not exist; they are all one.

Normally if I have to raise my hand, first the brain has to give the order, the order has to be carried to the hand and the hand has to act. In the language of normal human beings, these three things have to occur. But in divinity all the three are one and the same, and do not exist separately. So the very divinity is a miracle.

Many people come and ask me who created the world. There is no creator. Please be very clear: Existence created itself. The universe is a self-created entity. The very creation itself is a creator; it is intelligence, continually created.

It is a little difficult to understand. It is just 'creating'. The process is continuously going on because of its own intelligence. There aren't three separate things: creator, creation and created. There is just 'creating'; a self expression of intelligence. So in any miracle, the miracle itself is divine. The cause for the miracle is divinity, the happening is divinity and the result is also divinity.

If a person does not even have the desire to seek a guru, is there anything wrong with that person?

Something is seriously wrong! When you know that you don't know, you at least know that you don't know. When you don't know that you don't know, you don't even know that you don't know! When we don't know that we don't know, we don't search for a master. Only when we know that we don't know, we can start to know and when we start to know, the master happens in our lives.

Einstein became enlightened in the process of intensely studying Physics. Ouspensky became enlightened because of Logic and Mathematics. If we go deeply into any subject, we can become enlightened because all paths lead to the same goal. There is no need to do only *puja* or meditation to become enlightened.

Even if one does scientific research deeply to the very end, one can reach enlightenment. I always say, 'If one is logically logical, one goes beyond logic.' Ouspensky met his master, George Gurdjieff, in a casual way. At that time, Ouspensky was a mathematician of world repute and Gurdjieff was just a simple man. Some energy in Gurdjieff prompted Ouspensky to go up to him. He said, 'I feel that you know something that I do not know; can you teach me?'

Gurdjieff replied, 'You are the author of the wonderful book *Pentium Organ*; what can I teach you?' Ouspensky maintained that Gurdjieff had something that he could teach him.

Gurdjieff asked him to go to the next room and make a list of all the things he knew and did not know so that he, Gurdjieff, could teach him the things he did not know. With a pen in hand, Ouspensky tried to make a list of the things he knew, but could not make the list no matter how long or how hard he tried. He then realized that all his knowledge was only superficial and that he needed to search for a master.

As long as you believe the illusion that you know everything, you are in great danger. That is the reason you do not search for a master or spiritual teachings. If a man does not have a quest for even spiritual teachings, you can be sure that he does not even know that he does not know. That shows that he is in darkness without even knowing that he is in darkness. If you have had a glimpse of light at least once, then you will know that you are in darkness. If you have not had even this glimpse, you will not even know that you are in darkness.

A small story:

A man who was born blind went to a doctor and asked him if he could help him gain vision. The doctor examined him and said he would do an operation to give him vision and that he would be able to walk without his stick.
The blind man replied, 'Doctor, I understand two things. I understand that you will perform an operation. I understand that I will be able to see. But I do not understand how I will be able to walk without a stick!'
All his life he had used a stick to walk; he thought that the stick was related to walking itself and he could not understand how he would be able to walk without a stick. The doctor said, 'When you get your vision, you will understand.'

Similarly, only when you get a glimpse of light will you understand what type of darkness you are in. You will then start searching for a master or spiritual teachings.

When all the great masters are divine manifestations, why is it that you get attracted to a particular master?

Ramakrishna gives a beautiful example. The mother cooks the same fish in ten different ways for ten children. One she makes sweet, another is hot and spicy, yet another is fried. She cooks it in ten different ways to satisfy the taste and expectations of all her children. Actually, we each have our own mind set, our own expectations. The divine fulfills you in the way you want it. If you are well read, if you are intellectual, Shankara will appeal to you! If you have a passion for music and dance, Meera or Chaitanya who expressed through music and dance will appeal to you! The intellectual type may find singing and dancing foolish. Similarly, a man who is attracted to the ecstatic love of Meera and Chaitanya will think that it is a waste of time to sit and analyze intellectually all the time!

The person whose head is more dominant will be attracted towards intellectual avenues; the person who is heart oriented will be attracted towards devotional avenues and the one who is being oriented will be attracted towards meditation. There are so many paths and so many masters; each person is centered on a different energy. The person who constantly *thinks* is on the path of *gnana yoga* - the path of knowledge; the person who is centered on emotions is a *bhakti yogi* - following the path of devotion; for the person who is being oriented, who is silent and introverted, meditation is the path. So a person is attracted to the philosophy and the master based on his or her individual energy or mind set.

When you find the right master, something will suddenly happen between you and Him: a synchronicity; almost like falling in love! Actually, something more than that which cannot be expressed in words. It is not even falling in love, it is rising in love! With ordinary people, it is falling in love, but with the master, it can only be rising in love! You will find that he is expressing what you think, what you always wanted to hear. You will find that your heart falls in tune with him. So until this happens, continue the search. That is the right way and the only way of seeking.

Are we qualified to seek?

Ramana Maharishi answers this question beautifully by asking, Are you alive?' *(Questioner responds, 'yes')* That itself is the qualification! That is the qualification because life itself has been bestowed on you by the Divine. So that is more than enough to receive divine grace. Nothing more is required; the rest will be taken care of by the Divine.

The questioner asks about two masters, naming them.

Here is a question mentioning the names of two masters in India. What is the difference between them and what is the similarity?

Our mind is such that we always analyze for differences, similarities and what not. Masters are beyond our minds. When we try to analyze them, we always fail and fall. We can compare two objects. We can see what the similarities and the differences between two objects are, for example, these two vases. You can see the size, shape, front view, back view - everything about them. But in the case of masters, they are infinity; they are in an infinite dimension! How is it possible to see what the similarities and differences are between two infinities? The similarities and differences between two masters are the same as that between two infinities, that's all!

Yesterday you said that the difference between a disincarnate guru and a live guru was that a live guru can point you upwards. But nowadays there are so many gurus with such a large following that you can hardly have any contact with them. But a disincarnate guru may be able to guide you through dreams. Could you talk about this?

Yes, this is a major problem that modern day seekers face. Before I answer, I have to confess: here at least you get a chance to question me. You can find out from devotees in India how many people attend my programs there; forty or fifty thousand! I am myself not able to give them the opportunity to pose questions or even to come close! But let me explain it to you.

With live masters, whether they have a big following or a small following, whether you have close proximity to them or not, people have experienced that whatever thought or doubt they have in their mind is cleared by the master in some way or the other. Whenever the question is sincere, whenever it is a quest, you will find that the living master answers it in some way that will surprise you! The living master will guide you. This is more of a possibility with a living master than with a disincarnate master.

It is not impossible with a disincarnate master; it is possible; but we have forgotten the language in which they speak! Their language is too subtle. We need to drop our inner chattering in order to hear them. With a live master like me, you have a loudspeaker! So even if you have inner chatter, I can be louder than that! But disincarnate masters talk through a very subtle language. Be very clear, they are all the time talking to us. We can even call it communion. The problem is that it has become one-sided. We have forgotten how to listen to them; we have forgotten the language in which they speak. They speak in the language of silence. And we do not know that language.

You may know many other languages: English, Hindi, Tamil, Telugu, but not the language of Silence. Even when I say the word silence, you refer to the Oxford dictionary! The meaning given there is soundlessness. But that is not the meaning I want to convey. What I mean is a vibrant, live energy that is silent! You are not able to relate in that language. With a living master, you can understand what he has to say because he uses the language that you know. So the possibility of a living master being able to guide you is more than that of a disincarnate master.

Another problem is that with disincarnate masters you can always project your own ego and satisfy yourself. With a living master this is not possible as he continuously knocks your ego and destroys it.

How do you explain the phenomenon of individuals conveying God's words?

'Telepathy', 'I get the command': all these are an expression of our ego most of the time. Our own ego plays a double role. You speak for yourself and for Him also! You stand in front of the statue and pray to God, 'O God, give me your blessings!' And then you stand behind the statue and say, 'My son, I bless you!'

Most of the time, it is your intellect that plays both the roles. Sometimes, when you are too intense, you can even become schizophrenic! In India, this is what happens when some people start acting like God. They even start showing some special powers. They get into a hysterical state and start predicting the future. It seems as though God has descended on them. They are even worshipped. If God descends on a person, you will see only joy and bliss on their face. But these intuitive fortune tellers always appear to be tense and suffering. They are restless, agitated and keep shouting and creating strange noises. Such expressions can never be God.

When God descends, it is so beautiful, so ecstatic and blissful, because God is filled with love and energy. He radiates this love and energy. He radiates compassion, never restlessness. So don't cheat yourself; that is the only warning. Otherwise you can continue in any path that you choose.

Lifestyle Is Not Life

Lifestyle is all about the quantity of things that we possess. Life is all about the quality of our consciousness.

Lifestyle is related to the way in which we live, talk, dress, behave, earn our money and spend our money. All these are related to worldly life and are part of our life style. But life is much deeper than lifestyle. We are so caught up with our lifestyle, working so hard for our material needs that we forget that we have a life in addition to our lifestyle! We measure our life by our bank balance. Especially in today's world, we can get any service for money. There is nothing we cannot buy with money; so our entire life is reduced to monetary transactions. People start to believe that their whole being is nothing but their lifestyle. Many people come to me and tell me that whatever there was to achieve, they have already achieved, yet they feel dissatisfied. This is because they have achieved everything they want in their lifestyle, but not in their life. Life is not lifestyle, and lifestyle is not life.

When concerning ourselves with lifestyle, outwardly things are enough. But to achieve quality in life, we need more awareness and consciousness. In school, college and university, they teach us how to achieve a better lifestyle, but nowhere do they teach how to achieve a better life! The quality of our consciousness is never increased or supported by the so called education today. There lies the problem.

All our energy is spent and drained for the sake of a lifestyle. People are worried more about their name or their outward appearance. They have forgotten their 'being' which is the most important aspect of life. Lifestyle is all about getting a bigger and better bed, while life is about the quality of our sleep. In our pursuit of increasing the depth and quality of our bed we forget to increase the depth and quality of our sleep!

Why are we so concerned with lifestyle? Because we know nothing about life, we give so much importance to lifestyle. Lifestyle is a poor substitute for life. When I say lifestyle, I don't refer to worldly life alone. It is applicable to spiritual life as well. In the spiritual world, lifestyle refers to rituals. If too much importance is given to rituals and if we are too engrossed in them, we again miss the whole point of spirituality. In anything, the way we do it is lifestyle, but from *where* we do it, is life. When we do things from our being, with a complete understanding of life, then our lifestyle can be anything. It doesn't matter.

A small story:

Mullah Naseerudin was well known for his memory, or for the lack of it. He could never remember anything for long.
One day, he wanted to do three things when he got home. So, he tied three knots in his handkerchief to remind himself.
Once he got home, he did two of the things he had wanted to do, but he just could not remember what the third thing was! No matter how hard he tried to recollect, he could not remember. He sat up the whole night trying to figure out the third item on his list.
Early in the morning he suddenly remembered what the third item on his list was; he had planned to get a good night's sleep!

This is what happens when we are caught up with lifestyle; we simply miss life.

There are seven planes in which we lead our life. Recently I was reading a book about Hollywood movies. The author had conducted some research and found that all Hollywood movie stories could be classified into seven categories and each of these categories corresponded with the seven major emotions in us that are sex, worry, fear, attention-need, jealousy, ego and discontent. All stories are only adaptations or variations of these seven emotional scripts. I was surprised to see that the seven emotions listed were identical to the seven emotional states defined by Patanjali in his *Yoga Sutras*! Patanjali was a great saint of ancient India considered to be the father of *Yoga*. In our Life Bliss Program (LBP), we speak of these same seven emotions relating them to the seven *chakras* or energy centers in our body. Five thousand years ago Patanjali said that there are only seven major emotions with which we relate to the world. These are the seven planes that I referred to.

In Indian mythology, they refer to the seven *lokas* or worlds. These seven worlds don't really exist on the physical plane. They are only seven different ways of looking at the same world. When we wear green lenses, everything around us appears green. When we are centered on a particular emotion, we view the world through that particular emotion.

The first plane is that of sex. This is the space or plane from which we are born. On this plane, our lifestyle is filled with imagination and fantasy. If we are centered on this emotion, in any relationship, we will continuously feel that our partner has cheated us. The other person never cheats us; it is we who project our imagination and cheat ourselves. When we say we are looking for a life partner, we are actually looking for a dream partner. We are searching for a screen on which we can project our dreams and feel fulfilled. We are looking for a lifestyle partner not a life partner. So when we search for the partner we are constantly thinking, 'When I go to a party, I should have a partner who will glorify my lifestyle!' A life partner is one who is one with our being, our consciousness.

Life is energy; it is an expression of our inner consciousness; it is living in a way that gives us total satisfaction and fulfillment.

A small story from Einstein's life will explain this very well.

On his deathbed, Einstein was asked by a colleague what he would like to be in his next birth. Towards the end of his life, Einstein had become more of a mystic than a scientist. He had started believing in rebirth even though he was Jewish.
So to his colleague's question he responded that he would like to be reborn as a plumber. The colleague was surprised. Einstein told him that whatever there was to achieve in the outer world - money, name, fame and respect - he had achieved. He gave great truths to people. However his own life had become a lie. In his younger days he had wanted to be a plumber, but became a famous scientist instead. He had reached the top but did not know why he was there.

Einstein said, 'I discovered the greatest truth of the century for humanity, but my life has become a lie!'

If he had become a plumber, he would not have received any recognition, he would not have achieved a great lifestyle but he would have achieved the deep satisfaction of life itself. When life gives such deep satisfaction and fulfillment, one would not bother about lifestyle.

Lifestyle is related to our conditioning. If we are taught by models or actors that wearing jeans is necessary to a certain lifestyle, we will copy it. If we are shown that something else is in fashion, we copy that immediately. So lifestyle is the conditioning given to us by society. Lifestyle is societal but life is natural. Lifestyle is superficial, only skin deep, but life is the core of our being. If we keep in touch with our being, even our lifestyle will be more satisfying. Whatever style we may live in, we will be happy. But we always run after lifestyle thinking that it will give us happiness. Problems in life can never be set right by changing our lifestyle.

In my courses I ask, 'What is worry?' People always give me reasons for worry, instead of an explanation of what worry really is. If we work on reasons for worry, there is no end to it. Only if we work on the subjective experience of worrying, will we get rid of it. When we have a problem, and if we work on our lifestyle, it will never help. We need to work on life itself; create more awareness and consciousness. We can never relax if we work on lifestyle alone. If we do that, we will be able to relax only when we reach our grave. Even in the graveyard we will still be worrying about the kind of tombstone that should be erected over our grave! I hear that people here in America buy plots for their own burial while they are still alive. I believe plots overlooking the ocean are more expensive! When we are only bothered about lifestyle, naturally we keep running continuously, till we fall into our grave.

A small story:

In a city, the emperor came out for his morning walk from his palace. While he was walking, he met a beggar and asked him, 'What do you want?'

The beggar laughed at the emperor and said, 'You are asking me if you can fulfill my desire!'
The king was offended by the beggar and said, 'What is it? Just tell me and I can fulfill your desire.'
The beggar told the emperor, 'Think twice before you promise anything.'
The beggar was the emperor's past life master! He had promised in that life to the emperor that he would come and try to awaken the king in his next life. The king missed it in his past life and so the master had come again to try to awaken him this time at least.
But the king had forgotten it completely. Nobody remembers past lives. So he insisted that he will fulfill anything the beggar asked for.
The beggar said, 'My desire is a very simple one. You see this begging bowl. Can you fill this bowl with something?'
The emperor called one of his ministers and told him, 'Fill this man's begging bowl with money.'
The minister went and got some money and put it into the bowl; the money immediately disappeared. Again he dropped some money and again it disappeared. However much he poured into it, the begging bowl remained always empty.
The news went throughout the whole city and a huge crowd gathered near the palace. The emperor's prestige was at stake. He told his ministers, 'Even if the whole kingdom is lost, I am ready to lose it. I cannot be defeated by this beggar.'
Pearls, diamonds and emeralds were becoming exhausted.
Finally it was evening and the people were standing there in utter silence. The king fell at the feet of the beggar and admitted his defeat. He said, 'You have won, but before you leave just tell me what this begging bowl is made of?'
The beggar laughed at the emperor and said, 'There is no secret. It is made up of the human mind. It is nothing but human desire!'
This single understanding transformed the life of the king.

The mind is like a black hole. It simply takes in things endlessly and asks for more. We never relax or enjoy our lives. We postpone enjoyment. When we are studying, we say, 'I will enjoy life after marriage.' After marriage, we say, 'After I have children'. After children we say, 'After his education'; then we say, 'After retirement I will enjoy social security.' But by the time we retire, we are trained to run continuously. We have created within ourselves a mental set up that will never let us relax and enjoy anything.

I have seen in many cases that the son would have gotten married and even the grandson, but the old man will be going through the matrimonial column in the newspapers. He will be going through the entire paper from morning till night more thoroughly than even the editor of the paper! Why? Because he cannot sit with himself. We can sit with the television, the telephone, the paper, but never with ourselves. The capacity to sit with ourselves, the ability to be with ourselves silently in comfort is what I call life. Only this gives us a glimpse of real life. If we have nothing else to do, we start thinking: either planning or worrying. Here too we are bothered about lifestyle. Either we are collecting data, processing data, or conveying data! We are continuously running and running but never experiencing life.

If we really experience life fully, we will never have fear of death because life and death are not two separate things but are two sides of the same coin. If we have experienced life, we will realize that death is not an end to life but the climax of life, the peak of our lives - an intense experience; it is the intense energy of undergoing a transformation. The *Bhagavad Gita* (a discourse given by Lord Krishna to Arjuna) says that death is just like the changing of one's shirt. It is only a changing of our body into another one. And this changing of the body will lead to an inner transformation.

The second plane is one of fear. If you observe our whole lifestyle, it is actually based on fear. We are always afraid of something or the other. Even when we are enjoying something, we are afraid that we may lose that enjoyment. If we have experienced life to the core of our being, then we will know that we have nothing to be afraid of because we have nothing to lose. If something is to be lost then it is better to lose it fast. Anything that can be lost is not worth having!

We have so many types of fears: fear of losing material possessions; fear of losing physical and mental health; fear of losing one's loved ones and love; and then the fear of unknown happenings, including death, of which we know little. It is these things which bring about great unease and fear.

The ultimate fear we all have, is that of losing our identity, our ego. In many surveys, it has been established that while what most people fear is death, the second most common fear is that of public speaking! While these two fears may seem very different, they have a common thread - that of loss of ego. At death, we have no idea as to where we are going, what is going to happen to us. As a result, our ego feels threatened. Our ego is always used to having a solid identity and agenda. Death comes as a threat to it. In public speaking, the ego fears failure, of being shamed in public if the performance is not good enough.

In the meantime, society and religion keep instilling more and more fears into our system. The fear of sin, moral wrong-doing, of punishment in hell – all these are all drilled into us from childhood by those who wish to control us and our actions. None of these fears have any spiritual sanction. Spirituality never imposes morality on anyone. It always facilitates morality through deep awareness, never through compulsion or fear.

All these fears can only be overcome by facing them boldly. Fear is like a shadow; it follows us, stalks us. But one thing: the moment we turn around to face it, it disappears! That is the secret that we do not know. All we need to do is face the fear with understanding and awareness. The fear will simply dissolve. Then, we will understand that we were afraid of something that never had any truth in it.

The third plane is that of worry, what I call corrupted inner chattering. When our inner chattering or thoughts are corrupted, and they disturb our inner self, then worrying happens. All our worries are about our lifestyle. If we are centered on our lifestyle, we will be constantly worrying. The person who has a car will worry that he may not get the spare parts for it. The person who doesn't have a car will worry about not having one! We continuously come up with something to worry about. Worry becomes a crutch, a companion that we cannot do without.

Worries spring from the gap between our expectations and reality. Reality is happening as it should happen – in accordance with the flow of Existence. All we need to do is flow with it with deep reverence. But we start having our own expectations of how each moment should be. There starts the problem. The gap between the grand reality and our expectations, gives rise to a constant inner chatter of worry.

With increasing competition around us for everything - education, work, life partners etc - we find that we worry and feel stressful most of the time. Worry is almost our hallmark! When we worry in the office, we call it work; when we worry at home, we call it family issues; when we worry at the beach, we call it vacation. The body may be in different locations, but the mind is always on one focus - worry.

The interesting part is, we all believe that only *we* are special; only *we* have worries. That is not true. Every one has by and large the same worries; they are expressed in different ways, that is all. We worry with guilt about the past or with anxiety about the future. The past is buried and is history. The future is not at all under our control. The only meaningful thing is the present moment. If we understand this completely, we will stop worrying.

The next plane has to do with attention from others. Now our problem becomes a little more subtle; it becomes more emotional. As long as you are a lifestyle-based person, you will continuously ask for other people's attention. When we get attention from others, we feel happy; we are in an expanded mood. That is why people will give anything to become a celebrity. It gives them a boost; they get the attention of so many thousands of people. And all that attention gives them the energy. They feel more than life size! That is the reason why politicians feel so energetic when they are among their followers.

There is something called mob psychology. When you are in a crowd, you feel like you can do anything and get away with it! A person may scream 'Down, down' to the Principal of his college as part of a mob, but if we take that person out of the mob, he will simply shake with fear! This is the scale to see if you derive your energy from others or from yourself. If you are more energetic in a group, then your lifestyle is based on attention from others.

We always feel that the masses are led by leaders. The truth is, the leader does what the masses want. Leaders are the worst slaves because their energy is not based on themselves but on the attention of the masses. When the attention drops, they feel deprived and low. Similarly, when others tell us that we are good, we feel good. When others tell us that we are no good, we feel bad. Our opinion of ourselves is based on the opinion others have of us. If we are repeatedly told that we are 'a nobody', then we begin to feel like a nobody! We don't know who we are, and so we depend on others to tell us.

If you have had a solid experience with yourself, then you have knowledge about yourself. But if you are based only on your lifestyle, then you will depend only on certificates from others continuously, because lifestyle involves only the outer world. On the other hand, if you are based on life, you will get a deep satisfaction from anything that you do, not from what others say. When you get to know yourself, you measure yourself from your own opinion, and you will be living for life itself, and not for lifestyle.

How we build our self-esteem decides how our life is going to be. There are many things that we do because we need other people's approval, and equally many things we don't do because others may not approve. We feel the need to be politically correct to be approved of by society. In the end, we stop doing what we wish to do. We stop doing what gives us passion. We start living life for others, not for ourselves.

If we break out of this, buck the trend, and do what we are really passionate about, not caring what others may think of us, we are on the path to eternal happiness.

The fifth plane is that of comparing ourselves with others. We constantly compare what we have with what others have. We feel jealous about our friends, neighbors, colleagues and what not. If our colleague gets the latest car, our own car suddenly seems inadequate. We find the need to change our car every year, our house every three years and our spouse every five years! When we see what others have, we get jealous and immediately, our wants increase. Based on jealousy and greed, our wants increase. And there is no end to this. It will take us deeper and deeper into it. Jealousy is a terrible waste of our energy. It simply drains us. It is a wasteful emotion.

We are neither the best in anything nor the worst in anything. If we make people stand in a line depending on what they have and what they don't have, we will find that most of us will be somewhere in the middle. Yet, we are always struggling constantly to be number one and number two in something or the other. When we do this, we quickly become number one in reaching the graveyard! The seed to this number game is sown in our education system, when we start ranking our children. Once we rank the first three, does it mean that the rest of the class is useless? No! There is such tremendous potential in each child waiting to express! Only when we get out of this habit of ranking people, can global happiness start happening.

We must realize that each of us in unique. There is no scope to compare ourselves with others. Every moment spent in comparison is a moment wasted in our own growth.

The sixth plane is ego or high self-esteem. Imagining yourself to be higher or lower than what you really are is ego. Again, this is based on another's opinion of yourself.

Yesterday, a news reporter was asking me how I could have so much wisdom at such a young age. I told him that wisdom is not based on the incidents that happen in our lives, but based upon what we have learned from the experiences that happen. It does not depend on the number of incidents, but the number of things we have learned from the incidents. If we are aware, and if we have our eyes open, we don't even have to experience a whole lot of things. Life is too short to commit all the mistakes and learn from them. We can learn through sheer awareness. Suppose you touch a burning cigarette; you realize it burns. Then you touch a fireplace and see that also burns. Then you touch burning charcoal and realize that also burns. Next you touch a matchstick and find that it burns too! By the time you touch all types of fire, and realize that all types of fire burn, your body will be ready to be burnt! This is called learning from experience.

The other kind of learning is when you touch one kind of fire and realize that all types of fire burn. That is wisdom! Experience is based on lifestyle; wisdom is based on life. When you have sharp awareness, intelligence and the consciousness of being, every incident will reveal its truth to you. You become more aware of what is happening both inside and outside your being. You become more aware of what is needed to fulfill both your life and your lifestyle.

There are people who run and run to fulfill their ego. They run to achieve something, but once they achieve it, they feel like fools because it gives them no fulfillment. The other day, a man told me that when he first came to America, he had an agenda for himself.

He had a list of things to achieve, and he gave himself 20 years to do it. By God's grace, he had achieved all that he wanted to in just 8 years. Now, in spite of all that achievement, he felt a deep void in himself. He had achieved 'what' he wanted to achieve, but wondered 'what for' he had now achieved. He achieved only to get joy and bliss, but he felt he had not achieved that.

When you achieve for the sake of joy, the experience of that joy is temporary. It is mostly the joy of achieving. Once one achievement is completed, another project has to begin to keep the adrenalin flowing; otherwise you will fall into depression.

When you achieve and achieve, and find no joy in spite of it, it causes depression of success - the empty feeling that arises even after having achieved whatever is the societal idea of success. Almost every 'successful' person in the 'civilized' world suffers from this condition of depression of success. People in the so-called 'under developed' nations of the world, are still struggling towards material success, and their unhappiness results in depression of failure!

Depression of failure is in a way, better than depression of success. In depression of failure, there is hope that you may achieve your desires tomorrow, but depression of success leads you straight to the truth. Hope acts like a buffer with the truth. But when you have to face the truth directly, it hurts. When you realize there is nothing more to achieve and nowhere else to go, deep hopelessness happens in you. From there three paths are open to you. The first is the path of addiction – to drugs, alcohol, or even food. That is why you will see that depressed people start becoming obese. At least with drugs and alcohol, you may realize that they are in addiction. But when they are addicted to food, you will not even realize it. That is why there is such a high percentage of obesity in developed countries.

Here, in countries like America, people have achieved whatever there is to achieve in their lifestyle, but have left a huge void in achieving in their life itself. Life is sold for the sake of lifestyle. We sell our eyes to buy a painting, our tongue to buy good food, our legs to pay for dance classes! We have what we want - the lifestyle, but we do not have the life. The desired lifestyle is achieved, but not the core of life itself. Life becomes a rat race. The problem is that even if you win the rat race, you remain a rat!

To feed our egos, we continuously run; but in the end we feel like fools. When you run after something you want, you get it, but you find that the desire for that has disappeared! If you want a car very badly, you do everything to get it, but once you get it, you realize that it is no big deal after all. Very often you find that you have paid too much for the desire; invested too much time and energy. As long as we continue to run after our 'dream' lifestyle, we will continue to be under pressure, under stress. We will have no time to rest and enjoy our life. And this is what leads to deep discontentment.

Discontentment is the seventh plane. If we are based on lifestyle only, then we will experience only discontentment.

> *In the Mahabharata - the great Indian epic - there is a beautiful story about a king called Yayati.*
> *This king enjoyed all types of pleasures for a hundred years. But when Yama - the Lord of Death - knocked at his door, he was unwilling to open the door for Him. He pleaded with Him for an extension of an additional hundred years.*
> *Yama agreed, provided one of his sons was willing to die in his place. One of Yayati's sons agreed and Yayati was granted a hundred more years.*
> *At the end of another 100 years, Yama returned to claim him and again Yayati pleaded for a hundred more years. Again he was granted his wish with one more son dying in his place. This continued 10 more times, with Yayati getting continuous extensions.*
> *In the end, Yama said to him, 'You are pouring oil to put out the fire'. The moment he said that, Yayati had the first glimpse of enlightenment or satori.*

Yama told him that he was trying to pour oil to put out the fire! It means, he was going behind more desires to get out of the cycle of desires. How is that possible? Can you quench your desires by pouring more sensory pleasures onto them? Can you quench your discontentment by improving your lifestyle?

Lifestyle can never fulfill life. To be ready to die, you should have had a fulfilling life. Lifestyle can never get fulfilling because it is based on 'more'. Life can become fulfilling because it is based on 'what is'.

I always tell people: don't add more years to your life; add life to your years!

We can add life to our years in three ways: live in the present moment, have more awareness about what happens in the outer world, and be more deeply conscious of the changes in the inner world. These three ways will give you a glimpse of life, of the energy of life and an experience of *samadhi*.

If you are centered in consciousness, you will be centered in deep satisfaction all the time. When you are like this, at the level of sex, or the first plane, instead of fantasies, you will have a deep intimacy with your spouse. At the level of fear, there will be only understanding of the transient nature of things, never fear. At the level of worry, instead of corrupted inner chattering, you will have clarity of thought. Instead of psychological worrying, you will do effective chronological planning. At the level of attention, instead of drawing attention and energy from others, you will start radiating energy to others. At the level of self-esteem, instead of having low or high self-esteem, you will know who you are, and you will start expanding or flourishing in your own way. At the level of ego, you will work with complete awareness of yourself and others, and not fall into the trap of the ego. At the level of discontentment, there will be only deep fulfillment, never discontentment.

So many great masters have left their bodies at a very young age - like Shankara at 32, Vivekananda at 39, Ramakrishna at 50 and Yogananda as well. They had such deep satisfaction because they experienced life fully. If you are centered on lifestyle, you will work towards increasing your material possessions and life years. But if you are centered on life, you will continuously radiate energy and your material possessions and life years will increase as a natural by product.

There is no proof to support what I am telling you in science. It has to be experienced. It is beyond logic like all great things are. We cannot prove the presence of God through logic. The moment that is done, logic will become greater than God! God is great because He cannot be proved by logic. In the same way, life also is beyond logic; it is paradoxical. When we try to look at it logically, we miss life itself. Let these ideas sink into your being. Let this consciousness and awareness flower in yourself; let you experience life in eternal bliss – *nithyananda!*

Questions and Answers

When a person is very successful and then goes into depression, you said there are three ways of dealing with that. The first is addiction. What are the other two?

Yes. The first is addiction. The next is suicide - you kill yourself or you slowly die within; you become the living dead. The third method, which only a very select group of intelligent people choose, is that of meditation! These are the three paths to get out of depression. Meditation will make you go into the depression, know it, analyze it and then come out of it.

But isn't that very difficult, master?

Just change the programming in your mind, that's all! Instead of always saying it is very difficult, start saying it is easy. It is you who creates the word 'difficult' in your mind. In the beginning your mind will not accept that it is easy. It will resist. But if you go on telling yourself that it is easy, you will find that there is nothing to it and that it *is* actually easy.

Ramana Maharishi - an enlightened master from South India - says so beautifully, 'So easy this *atmavidya* – knowledge of the soul; so easy this enlightenment!' His followers ask him how he can say that it is easy. To this he replies that only to achieve in this outer world, to have a good lifestyle, you need to work very hard. But to achieve in the inner world, you only have to relax and be quiet; that is enough! All that you need to do is just *be*.

We have been trained to achieve so many difficult things that we have forgotten how to achieve the simple things! Just look in. You are not so poor that you cannot even address your own mind with good words, cannot even speak kindly to yourself. Of course you can!

To do meditation, stillness of the mind is necessary. They say pranayama - controlled breathing techniques - helps a lot.

'Stillness of mind', *'pranayama'*, all these are big words which create more complications. Meditation is very simple. Now, as you are sitting, just become aware of your boundary. Not going where *you* are not, is meditation. Being where you *are* is meditation. Usually what happens is that when you are here, you are thinking of your home. When you are at home, you are thinking of the evening discourse. At the discourse, you are thinking of when you can go back. At home you are thinking of the next day's office work. At the office, you are planning the evening outing. When you are outside, you start thinking of home again. Our mind is never where our body is. When we can be completely where we are, we are in a meditative mood. So being in the present, living with awareness and consciousness, is what I call meditation.

We are always disturbed by too many words and ideas. Just relax and be where you are. Feel the ground, feel how you are sitting, and feel all the parts of your body. Just experience the present. By just being totally in the body, you will start experiencing life. Because this idea is so simple, it is very difficult to understand.

All our lives we are used to thinking about the past or future. It is very difficult to come out of it.

If you are used to living in the past or in the future, don't be bothered by it. When you say it bothers you, it means that it is not your nature! So why do you want to do something that is not true to your nature? Here is a small logical example: when you have a headache, you try to come out of it. You take some medicine to come out of it because headache is not your normal nature. In the same way, if worrying and thinking about the past and the future gives you pain, then obviously, it is not your nature! So stop worrying! Associate yourself only with living in the present.

Let us say you have come from Hyderabad and settled here for the past 30 years. As you have had no practice, you have forgotten how to speak Telugu. Suddenly if somebody starts speaking to you in Telugu, will you not remember? In the same way, bliss and living in the present is a language more close to you than your own mother tongue. Up to the age of 7, you were in that state. So start reclaiming that forgotten language, that forgotten state!

Life Is An Eternal Celebration

Life is an eternal celebration! Once we understand each and every word of this statement, then only will we be able to understand the whole subject.

Life! What is really the meaning of life? Eastern mystics always say, 'Life has some goal.' Western philosophers always contradict this. They say life has no goal. In the east, almost all mystics, from Buddha to Krishna, Mahavir to Nagarjuna, Shankara, Kabir to Tulsidas, all the saints, all the seers always emphasized that life has some goal. In the West, almost all philosophers who have analyzed the intellect, who have studied logic, said, 'Life has no goal.'

Somebody once asked me, 'Master, does life really have a goal? What is the truth?' I answered saying, life has no goal, but it has purpose! Goal is one thing, purpose is another. We need to understand the word 'purpose'. Goal means, we travel to reach something. Life becomes a road on which we travel in order to achieve something. Purpose means the *very road* is the purpose! It is not that we traverse through life to attain something. The very *life* is that 'something'. It is not a way; it is a goal in itself.

A small story:

A few friends were sitting and chatting over a cup of coffee. The first man says, 'I know a man who has spent every single one of his evenings at home for the last 30 years since he got married.' The other man replies, 'Oh! This is what I call love, real love for your wife.' The third man says, 'You call that love? The doctor calls it paralysis!'

Most of the time, our lives are nothing but a paralysis. We don't make our decisions with our consciousness. Decisions happen without our consciousness - as if we are in paralysis and can't exercise our consciousness. If they happen by our conscious choice, because of our conscious decision, only then is it life. It is life only when we decide to live it. Until the moment we decide to live, it can never be called 'life'.

There is an aphorism in the *Upanishads* which says, 'A man who decides to live is not affected by any of the *karmas* (unfulfilled actions).'

We need to understand what *karma* is; then we will be able to understand this one line. *Karma* means the conscious choices which we make. Conscious choices, which we continually make is what comprise *karma*. Our lives are nothing but the totality of our conscious choices, which we continuously make. Whether we want to or not, directly or indirectly we are choosing every time. Someone else does not choose for us. It is we who choose. It is continuously our choice, our decision. We may think somebody else decides. But it is always us who decides.

With a small example we can understand this basic truth. If somebody criticizes us, we choose to get offended. If somebody praises us, we choose to be flattered. Because this may be a habitual pattern for us, we may choose it unconsciously and so we don't even realize that we choose it. But nobody else ever chooses for us. It is always our choice. Because it has become our habit, we forget that we are choosing. Every time somebody criticizes us, we choose to be upset. Every time somebody praises us, we choose to be flattered. It is nobody else's choice but our own. We can decide either way. Sometimes when somebody criticizes us, we can choose to not get offended; we can choose to remain calm, relaxed, collected.

Continuous choices, our choices, are what is called 'life'. All our choices every minute, put together, decide our life. If we don't make decisions, if we let incidents decide the direction of our lives, then this becomes 'paralysis'. Our lives are, as of now, nothing but a series of paralyzed situations. It is only when we decide to live our lives without any interruption, without any guidance or outer forces, without any outer situations or decisions being forced on us, we decide to really live. As long as we don't understand life is our choice, our living is paralyzed.

Let us say that you get a new car, a Mercedes Benz; you get into the car and start the vehicle. You are driving around for a while. After going around the block, when you come back to your portico and your garage, you need to stop the car. Until that point you knew everything: how to start, how to operate the car, how to turn right, and left, but now you don't know how to stop. If you don't know how to stop, *you* will not be driving the car; the *car* will be driving you! In the same way, *you* are not living, *life* is living you. If you don't know how to stop the car, you are just paralyzed.

Put simply, matter is living the energy, not energy living the matter. There are two things in us: our being – energy, and our outer life – matter. If we consciously decide, if our energy decides to live without being affected by outer situations, without being touched by outer things, we start really living; our consciousness shines. Otherwise, matter lives through us; we do not live through matter. Life can be about living or it can be about paralysis. It can be either.

Understand this small thing: normally, if matter lives our life, our importance grows if matter grows. Our importance is nothing but our wealth. If we have more cars, more bungalows, greater bank balance, we get more importance. Our value increases with matter, with the things we possess. As I said earlier, our being is energy. So in this mode of life, energy gains value through matter.

If you visit the Ramana ashram in Tiruvannamalai in South India, you can find small, old coconut shells, a piece of furniture, a small staff, being worshipped by thousands of people. That small staff, the old coconut shell, the small piece of furniture, all these have been touched by Bhagwan Ramana Maharishi, an enlightened person. So they are worshipped.

This is the second thing we need to understand. In Bhagwan's case, though the matter may seem small and of no apparent value, merely because it has been touched by his enlightened energy, the value of this matter has been greatly increased! In the ordinary material world, matter adds value to us. But in the case of these enlightened beings, having lived consciously, *they* add value to matter!

A small story:

A rich old widow got married for the second time. One day her husband did something that upset her. The rich widow got very angry and started to shout, 'But for my money this furniture would not have been here. But for my money this house would not have been here. But for my money you would not have such a big car. But for my money you would not have all these comforts. You are misbehaving with me!' Her husband calmly replied, *'But for your money I would not have been here. Your value is nothing but your money.'*

We are judged by the paraphernalia we surround ourselves with. Because of the paraphernalia that surrounds us, we get value. Matter therefore adds value to energy in this case. In the case of people who live consciously, people who have become enlightened, value is added to matter by their energy. Whether matter should gain value through energy or whether energy should gain value through matter is our choice.

A man who is paralyzed is always weighed by matter. For a man who really lives, even his matter is valued by his energy like how *Bhagwan's* belongings were valued. When a conscious man touches anything, it becomes holy. Even small things like an old coconut shell, a piece of wooden furniture or a staff, even those things become objects of worship. These men receive respect because they lived consciously. Energy guided their lives. Conscious decisions guided their lives. When we actually decide to live, when we consciously decide to live, life starts happening to us.

A great enlightened master George Gurdjieff who was from the west, was a gift to the world. He once said, 'All of you do not have a soul. It has to be created.' In a way that is not the truth. But by saying this, he means to inspire us. The words used are part of a technique. He wants to imply that only when we start to live consciously, the soul is created! Actually when we start living consciously, only then is the soul expressed. Even if we have a soul, when we don't make conscious decisions, it doesn't matter. How does it matter whether we have a soul or not, if we don't live consciously? If we don't use it, whether we have it or not, is immaterial. The soul expresses itself and energy expresses itself only when we make conscious decisions. Conscious decision-making does not refer to decisions relating to our jobs or marriage or our lifestyle. It is not related to just big decisions. It is related to every moment of our lives.

Even while making ordinary decisions like sitting in a chair, sit consciously. Feel the comfort of the chair consciously. Sit not only consciously, but also listen to things happening around you; see the things happening around you consciously. When you do this, material things will no more create an impression on you!

When we don't decide consciously, *samskaras* are created. The word *samskara* should be understood. It is a beautiful Sanskrit term. If one understands the idea, then one can grasp the meaning. In English there are words - 'imprint' or 'impression', but I am not satisfied with these words; the closest words that can translate *samskaras* are perhaps 'emotion filled memories'.

Let us see how we can understand this concept. As we live, whenever we act, a print of that is created in us, a hangover of that activity is created in us: that is *samskara*. *Samskara* means that if, for instance one continuously drinks coffee, the idea or habit of that is imprinted in one's mind. *Samskara* has a powerful potential energy to make one repeat the action. People come and tell me, 'Master, at exactly 10 pm every evening, wherever I am, I am reminded of drinking. I am unable to control myself. I find myself being pulled towards the bar and then my mind makes a decision and I go to the bar.' That is a *samskara*.

Samskaras are powerful. It is almost like gun powder sprinkled or spread throughout our being. At certain times they affect us strongly; it is almost as if we have no choice to do what we want to do. They act on us making us do the same thing again and again. The more we repeat our actions the deeper the *samskaras* get inserted into our very being. It is a vicious circle. 'Doing' makes a *samskara* and repeating the action makes it deeper. In other words creating *samskaras* makes one do things, and doing things makes the *samskara* deeper.

When one understands *samskara* then one will understand what life actually is. As of now, we don't live, only our *samskaras* live through us. Imprints are made in our minds by social conditioning, by the way we are brought up in society, by our unconscious decisions; whatever is done creates a set of *samskaras* and these are living through us now. It is not as if we are living *samskaras*. If we cannot stop any habit, the habit starts living through us. If you eat what you want, it can be said that you are eating. If you eat without control of your mind, the food is eating you. First you start to drink a little alcohol; soon, alcohol will drink you. That is how *samskaras* work.

Initially, we create *samskaras;* later on *samskaras* live our lives. As of now our lives are pure *samskara*, habits. As I always say, the word 'habit' is the right word. If you drop the 'h', 'a bit' is left, if you drop the 'a', 'bit' is left. If you drop the 'b', 'it' remains. Only when you drop the 'i' will it die! The habit survives because of us, our mind.

When we decide to live consciously, life happens to us. Don't think life happens to us when we are born. When we are born, only the seed, the potentiality of life is given to us, never life itself. When we decide to live consciously, only then are we really born, or rather reborn. In Eastern mysticism there is a word *dhvija* which means a man who decides to be consciously reborn, a man who decides to give birth to himself consciously through strong intention of living consciously. If you are initiated into meditation, if you take somebody as your master and you are given a technique, you are called *dhvija* – reborn.

There is something called a *Gayatri mantra*. Once a person is initiated with the *Gayatri mantra* he is said to be a *dhvija* or twice-born. Being initiated with the *Gayatri mantra* does not mean that you become religious; no! The Hindu philosophy, rightly called *sanatana dharma* - a philosophy, a spiritual culture, a world-view and a way of life that is open to, and welcoming of all people without discrimination - is a beautiful system which makes no effort to condition anyone. So understand that the *Gayatri mantra* is not a religious thing or any baptizing. It says: *let me meditate on the ultimate consciousness which awakens my intelligence. Let that intelligence help me to meditate on it.* That is all! The *Gayatri* has no idea of form, of any god or goddess, or an idea that it is attempting to engrave in one's consciousness. One is simply initiated.

Take this instance of a man, more than 70 years old who has lived in the same forest throughout his life. A young man, a person new to the forest comes to him and asks, 'Sir, how can I cross this forest. Please help me.' So the old man starts giving directions, 'Go one kilometer further. You will find a lion. Then take a left, travel three kilometers and you will find a big snake. Then escape from the snake, go three kilometers and you will find a valley. Cross the valley, go four kilometers and you will find a river. Cross it and you will reach the other side.'

Is this guidance going to help the young man? No! Instead of that if he is given a torch, the torch will give him a clear view of the road and that will be enough. The guidelines are of no help because the forest is continuously changing. Life is more like a forest. It is difficult to live by guidelines, by rules. We need understanding, clarity. All we really need is a torch and we will each be able to find our own unique path to the other side of the forest.

When you are given a set of concepts, beliefs, it is very much like spoon feeding. When you have been told to follow a set of beliefs, you cannot live in a natural way. Most of us are given just an ideology - only a set of guidelines; go this way, that way, you will find this; you will find that. When we go there and don't find what we are looking for, we feel, 'What is this? There is nothing here, or did I go the wrong way. What should I do now?' We get stuck at some point or other. Instead, if we are given guidelines, if we are given a torch, we will see that we can walk through life by ourselves. Initiation is like giving you a torch.

The *Gayatri* does not belong to any religion. It is just a decision to live consciously. The emphasis on consciousness is given to you through it. You are made to understand what consciousness actually means. The *Gayatri mantra* has no other religious connotation attached to it. Of course later on some perceptions may have been added, but originally it meant only one thing - a conscious decision to live consciously. When we start living consciously, life happens to us; we are reborn, *dhvija*. A man who is reborn in this way is a conscious being - a man who decides to live consciously. In the *Upanishad* they call him a *paramahamsa* - a man who decides to live consciously; one who goes beyond *karmas*.

When we decide to live consciously, our *samskaras* do not have any role to play in our lives. Our *samskaras* can never play any role in our lives then, because *samskaras* are from the past. Our being is in the present; *samskaras* are more or less like ghosts. The past is dead!

When I was wandering in India, I had a nice time. For more than nine years I traveled. I wandered throughout India, mostly by foot. I always stayed in graveyards! If you see my pictorial biography, you will see many photographs of me in different graveyards. People ask me why I stayed in graveyards. I tell them, 'First of all, I never needed to make any reservations there! Secondly, almost every village has a graveyard. Thirdly, nobody stays there! All the inhabitants are dead; they never disturb others.' Others ask me, 'Master, weren't you bothered by ghosts?' I said, dead people never disturb others; only living people disturb others.

Ghosts are lower level beings. Ghosts are more or less like *samskaras*. If we don't have the awareness to live consciously, they take advantage and rule us. If we are able to live consciously and make conscious decisions, they have no ability to live through us as they are lower than us. As long as our consciousness is awakened, as long as our individuality is awakened, as long as we have made the decision to live, neither ghosts nor *samskaras* can disturb us; because both are dead and are from past memories..

The power of ghosts does not lie in the ghosts themselves; it lies in the way we empower them. It is our belief in them that makes them powerful, much like the character, Vali, from the great Hindu epic *Ramayana*. Vali had been granted a boon that anyone facing him in a fight would lose half his power to him. That is how it works with ghosts; when we start believing in them, they get half our power. Otherwise neither *samskaras* nor ghosts have any value.

Many people come and tell me, 'Master, I know smoking is a bad habit but I am unable to stop because it has become a habit.' One man came and told me, 'Master, last week I read a book of all the bad things that happen to us when we smoke; not only the effects of smoking but also the health problems caused by second-hand smoking. I read a big book about smoking and then I stopped.' So I asked him, 'Oh, that is good. So you have stopped smoking?' The man replied 'No, no, master! I have stopped reading those kinds of books!'

Many times we consciously understand that something is wrong but we say, 'It has become a habit. I am unable to stop.' I tell you, habits have no value. If we decide to be conscious, habits have no power over our consciousness, . It is just your conscious choices that have made the habit deep. When we decide to live consciously, our choices can be changed. That is why it is usually said, that a man decides to become enlightened. I use other words. I say, 'Man *chooses* to become enlightened!'

Buddha became enlightened on his birthday. *Buddha Purnima* is the day on which he was born and the day on which he became an enlightened; of course years later, but on the same day. There was a question asked of Buddha, 'Master, how did you become enlightened on the same day as your birthday? How did that happen?' Buddha replied, 'When I say I have become enlightened, don't think something special has happened to me. I decided to live out my natural state that is enlightenment. That is all! It is just a conscious decision. So when I take such a decision, I can consciously choose, 'Oh! It is my birthday; it is a good day. Let me live out my enlightenment.'

We need to understand only one line of an aphorism from the Hindu scriptures. It is a secret, the master key of one's own enlightenment. **When you decide consciously, you simply express your enlightenment.** When we decide consciously, we can simply walk over our *samskaras* because neither our *samskaras* nor ghosts have any value as they are. It is only we who give power to them.

A small story:

A man used to come home late every evening after having drunk to his heart's content. His wife asked her friend to give her some ideas, some suggestion to stop this habit in him. The friend suggested, 'Since he needs to pass through the city graveyard today, maybe you can hide yourself near the graveyard and when he comes by, you can frighten him by making some strange sounds. Then there might be a chance that out of fear of crossing the graveyard, he will not come home late. Once he starts coming home early, naturally he will not go to the bar and his drinking habit will drop. Try this technique.'

The wife decided to do what her friend had advised her to do. She prepared herself by putting on makeup, black clothes and carrying a small pot with fire, so that she could create some smoke for effect. After she was through with her preparations, she went to the graveyard and hid herself behind a stone. Soon, her husband came by. When he walked by, she jumped in front of him and started to wail, in her strange dress, with all her paraphernalia.

The man stood unperturbed looking at her. He took her hand in his, shook it and said, 'Don't you recognize me? I live with your sister!'

It is our being which gives respect to ghosts and *samskaras*, which are one and the same. That is why they say the ego is like a ghost. If we give it importance and value, it will be present. If we don't give it respect, it will be absent. There is a beautiful word in Sanskrit - *maya*. *Maya* is that which is not there, but poses to be as though it is there; that which is not there, but continuously appears to be there. Ghosts and *samskaras* are only alive as far as we are concerned. As far as our unconscious living is concerned, ghosts and *samskaras* are our life. In reality, they don't have any solid existence.

When we consciously decide to live our life, we start living. Life happens to us when we consciously allow it to happen. So start living life and you will see that life happens to you. Until then, you do not know the meaning of life; you do not know even the word 'life'!

The next word is 'is'. Life 'is' an eternal celebration. Life 'was' never an eternal celebration. Life 'will' never be an eternal celebration. Life 'is' an eternal celebration. We all have an idea, almost in every religion, in all philosophies - that the past was golden. In Hinduism they call it *Satya Yuga*. In Christianity, they call it the Garden of Eden in which Adam and Eve lived. In Buddhism, they call it the yoga of *dhamma*, the age of *dhamma*. In every religion, in every sect, in every culture, they have an idea that there was a time when life was an eternal celebration; that there was a time when everything was as it should be – ideal! Every religion, every cult has such an idea that in the distant past, 'once upon a time', things were perfect.

This idea of *satya yuga*, the garden of Adam and Eve, *dhamma yuga*, is just our idea.

Let me tell you about a small incident.

Archeologists found a stone inscription from the ancient civilization of Mesopotamia that flourished 6000 years ago in the Middle East. If one read it they would be amazed by the similarity between it and today's newspapers, today's editorials. The inscription said, 'Once upon a time, people used to be moral, people used to be disciplined. Now, no son listens to his father; wives disobey husbands, husbands are unfaithful to their wives; this is a time without morals. We need to do something to revive moral behaviour among people.' Five thousand years ago, the Hindu epic *Bhagavatam* says that '*Kali*, the evil spirit, has entered the world. Now, a father tries to misbehave with his daughter, a mother tries to have a relationship with her son.'

There was never a time when life was heaven. Only in this instant can we make life a celebration. It was always as it is now. But we feel that life was a celebration in the past. When people reminisce, they always say, 'We had a golden childhood.' We always talk about our 'golden childhood'. Did we feel that at that time? No!

Do you know why we take photographs? Because only in photographs can we enjoy life, never when we live in those real scenes. I always find wherever we go, people continuously take photographs. I ask why they take photographs missing the real moments. But they don't understand. Then when the moment is past, they look through their album at the photographs and reminisce, '*Oh, it was so nice. We went to this place; it was so joyful. See how happy we were at that time.*'

When we are actually taking the photographs, we don't enjoy the moment. I have seen that when people go sightseeing, they are so bothered about taking photographs that they never enjoy the things around them. They are so preoccupied with covering the whole place with their camera. They are continuously obsessed about taking pictures, about the correct angles to take the best pictures. Their eyes turn blind because they don't look around at things in the present and enjoy. We try to make even the present moment part of the past. We can enjoy only the past, so we let the present moment pass. We have lost the habit of enjoying the present. When we are there, we don't have the time to enjoy ourselves. When the event has passed us by, we enjoy the event as past. The mind is habituated to only enjoy the past. This is a mental habit.

Psychologists say that for nine months while in our mother's womb, we never had any responsibility, never had any work and never had to do anything. We were totally taken care of, alone, joyful, independent of all bondage and responsibilities. We were in bliss. We enjoyed our aloneness which is our true nature. That imprint, the *samskara*, the hangover of that period when we lived in the womb, makes us feel that the past is great. The memory of the feeling of that time makes us think that the past was great.

The past was never grand. There is a beautiful word *tataka* in *Pali*, the language of Buddha, which means 'to be at ease', meaning that only in the present can one be living. This is the only moment that can be lived. It is just our belief that the past was great; that there was a time in our lives when everything was well. If we scan that time in the past and consciously see, then we will understand that at that point in time we were much in the same mood. We always say, 'College was the best time of my life.' But when we were living it, did we say that about it?

So understand the relevance of this word. Life *was* never an eternal celebration. Life *will* never be an eternal celebration. Life *is* an eternal celebration. It is the present 'is' which makes us happy or sad. If one is enjoying the past or future, then realize that one is enjoying only the *samskara*, the hangover. One is living with a ghost. As the man said, *'Didn't you know? I have been living with your sister for so long.'*

We are living with ghosts if we think the past was eternal, the past was a celebration, or the future will be a celebration. The 'is-ness' or *thathata* is lost. This is a beautiful word. When we live in the is-ness, things are totally different. To live in the is-ness we need sensitivity. We need life.

The next word is 'eternal'. Life is an eternal celebration. The word 'eternal' needs to be understood. We always understand this word as being the past, present and future, all three put together.

> *There is a short story from Sufism which will help us understand the meaning of the word 'eternal':*
> *There was a Sufi master called Abdullah. He was a mystic who lived throughout his life in nithyananda - eternal bliss. He used to be continuously happy and blissful from morning to night, wherever he was. The Sufis drank wine, so even when he drank he was happy. When a person drinks we see their original face. People are all smiles and happiness till they have a drink. After a drink all their stupidity is revealed. In Buddhist or Zen monasteries, one is made to drink before one enters a monastery. By this they read one's unconsciousness,*

what one is; who one is. So even when Abdullah had drunk wine, he was happy; he was in ecstasy, even his unconscious mind was in ecstasy. One day somebody asked him, 'Master how are you continuously happy? What is the technique you practice?' His reply was beautiful. He said, 'I never decide to be joyful for days in advance. When I get up in the morning, I ask myself, 'Abdullah do you want to be happy, do you want to be blissful today or do you wish to be in sadness? My mind always tells me that I want to be joyful. Then I tell myself, 'Okay, then be happy; then be joyful.' Simple! I only decide for that day, not for the next day. I never decide for eternity.'

What would we do if we were asked this question? We would decide for eternity. One may not remember tomorrow. One might reason that it might be better to decide to be eternally happy this instant. But that is not going to work. Our idea of eternity is totally different. Abdullah says, 'Everyday I decide, as soon as I wake up in the morning. I decide that today I want to be happy. I do not bother with the next day.'

People ask me two or three questions when I relate this story. The first question is, 'Master, he has no other responsibility; that is why he can afford to be happy. We have so many responsibilities, how can we be happy, blissful?'

We must understand one thing. If one starts worrying, will one's responsibilities be sorted out or taken care of? If we think that by being worried, by being sorrowful, by being morose, we will be able to carry out our responsibilities in a better way, then we can cry as much as possible; be in sorrow as much as possible; be as miserable as one wants, but is it going to work well? Is it going to give us any solutions?

If one has ten problems, by worrying one creates the eleventh problem. I tell people to decide as soon as they wake up. When you wake up early in the morning, call yourself by your name. It is a strange thing, but when you call yourself by your name, the ghosts or *samskaras* with which you associate yourself get disconnected. As long as you think of yourself as 'Abdullah', you cannot call yourself 'Abdullah'. Generally, you never associate yourself with your name; you only associate yourself with *samskaras* or ghosts. When others call your name, it is an unconscious process, but when you call yourself by name it is a conscious process.

Gurdjieff says that for self-realization, it is the best *mantra* or chant. We do not know the power of our name. If ten people are sleeping in one room and one person's name is 'Ram', when you call that name the other nine will not respond; only Ram will respond. Our name penetrates through our being. If we disassociate ourselves from our name, we completely disassociate ourselves from our *samskaras*. So according to Abdullah, it is a powerful technique. He says, I call myself *Abdullah, Abdullah, Abdullah, what do you want, joy, or sorrow and misery?* When we call ourselves by our name we create distance between ourselves and our *samskaras*. We create an understanding that we are not our *samskaras*. When we understand that we are not our *samskaras*, half the job is done. Then ask yourself whether you want to live joyfully or in sadness and misery; after all we already know what is going to happen in the next 24 hours.

Our lives are nothing but a simple routine. The same cup, whether lifted by the left hand or right, is not going to change anything; not even the temperature of the coffee in it will be affected. We already know what our routine is. We need to give ourselves a chance to live the same routine in a mood of bliss. Then we will realize that every moment of our lives can be penetrated, can be lived in bliss.

When bliss enters our lives, it transforms…*sat chit ananda*. In Sanskrit they use these three words to describe the same phenomena *sat* means 'truth', *chit* means 'consciousness' and *ananda* means 'bliss'. When *ananda* occurs, the effects of truth and consciousness can be felt in our lives. When consciousness enters our lives, the effects of truth and bliss manifest themselves. When any of these enter our lives, our life is transformed. There is an alchemy that happens in our lives. Especially when one tries to live their life in *ananda*, when we try to penetrate our life with *ananda*, miraculous transformation can happen. We do not know the miracles that can be performed by living in *ananda*. When *ananda* enters, consciousness enters. In consciousness, thousands of things can happen in our lives. One should attempt living one entire day consciously.

The next thing that people ask me is, 'If my mind decides to be in misery, what should I do?' Live in misery, what is wrong with that!

Abdullah said, 'If my mind decides to live in misery, it is perfectly alright. It enjoys misery; that is why it decides to be in misery.' If we don't enjoy misery, we will never choose misery.

Actually, we enjoy misery and that is why we choose it. We have our own vested interest in all our diseases, in all our miseries; otherwise we would not bring them into our lives. It is our decision. We often forget that we invited misery, and we also forget how we invited it. When we fall sick, we are attended to. So the need for attention makes us feel sick. Children use this technique. If we don't give them attention, they come to us with a headache, stomach pain, or a slight fever. It is a mental habit. So if one decides to have misery, decides to have sadness, enjoy it! There is nothing wrong; it is perfectly alright. But enjoy it consciously. If we understand this story, then we will understand the meaning of the word 'eternal'. Eternal does not mean the past, present and future. Eternal means only one thing - the present. It means living in this moment which is the only thing available to us.

Abdullah said, 'I don't decide ahead for two continuous days, because if I decide for two days I will never practice it.' Decide for each day. Every morning when you wake up just ask yourself, 'Ram, what do you want? Do you want to be in sorrow, or do you want to be joyful? If your mind says, 'I want to be blissful,' then be blissful, be joyful. It is your conscious decision. Your conscious decision can work miracles.

Buddha says, 'If you drop one handful of lime in a pool of muddy, dirty water, within an hour all the dirt will settle. The water will become crystal clear.' In the same way, conscious decisions are like lime, which can clear the dirt or mud from the pool of our mind. Just add a little conscious decision and you can see the miracles done by this conscious decision. Conscious decisions can lead to the ultimate alchemy or transformation in our systems. In other words, a great transformation can take place by our conscious decisions. So 'eternal' or *nithya* does not mean past, present or future. *Nithya* means the present only, never the past or the future.

The present is *nithya*. If we think 'eternal' means past, present and future, we will not be able to do anything because we have no hand in the past and have no hand in the future; we have our hand only in the present. So if 'eternal' is understood as meaning the past, present and future, then we have no decision to make; we have nothing to do. If we understand 'eternal' to mean the present, only then do we have something to do. So understand, 'eternal' means present. According to Abdullah's technique, decide only for twenty-four hours, not more than that. Even that is too much! You should flow with just the moment! Then you flow with Existence!

Trust – Even If You Are Exploited

A small story:

There was a Zen master who lived alone in a forest. One day, while he was meditating, a thief entered his house. The thief threatened the master at knife point and told him to part with all his valuables or to be prepared to die. The master said, 'There is nothing in my house. Let us both search.' They searched the house but couldn't find a thing. The thief was very upset and disappointed. The master then told him that there were a few coins in a pot which he had saved for his next meal and that he could have them. The thief took the coins and as he was about to leave, the master also handed him a sweater as it was very cold outside. The thief accepted it with glee. Just as he was leaving the house, the master asked him to thank him for what he had given him. The thief did so and left.

After a few weeks, the thief was arrested in connection with another theft. The police brought him to the master's house as the thief had also confessed his previous theft. When the police asked the master to identify the thief and confirm the theft, the master very calmly told the police that the stranger had visited his house and that he himself had given him some coins and a sweater. He also went on to say that the stranger had also thanked him for the gifts. Hearing this, the thief was shocked. After serving the sentence for his other theft, he came back to the master, fell at his feet and became his disciple.

This is not a story but a real incident.

A similar incident occurred in the life of Ramana Maharishi. Two burglars broke into Ramana Maharishi's ashram. To their dismay, they could find nothing but a few vessels. Just before leaving the place, in their frustration, they hit the master with a crowbar. They were arrested within a week and brought before Ramana Maharishi to be identified. Ramana Maharishi calmly said, 'Some people throw flowers on me, some compose verses about me and some criticize me. As the burglars had none of these, they substituted with the crowbar.'

These two incidents may sound far-fetched and illogical to us. But the fact is that these are real incidents and have tremendous meaning in them. How can we practice these things in our daily life? We think that it is impossible for us to do the same, and that only enlightened masters could be this way. We always separate ourselves from the masters. It is only an excuse for not attempting to follow their teachings.

Why was Jesus crucified by the Jews? They just wanted to escape from him. Jesus was preaching the Gospel, but people found it too difficult to practice the Gospel. His preaching demanded too much from them. People were not ready for it. When we are not ready to follow the teachings of an enlightened master, there is no point in worshipping him as we are only crucifying him. Just by decorating your wall with his photograph and offering *arati* (worship with lit camphor) to it, you will reach nowhere. We may accept that he is great and feel that he deserves the *arati* and worship. But we are not ready to follow his teachings. Only people who have not given a little space to spirituality in their lives come to conclusions like this. Worshipping is no different from crucifixion if we do it with this attitude. Hanging the master on the wall and hanging him on the cross are one and the same. Whenever we worship him without following his teachings, it is a subtle crucifixion.

If worshipping is done in a cunning way to escape my teachings, remember that hanging me on the wall and hanging me on the cross is one and the same. If worship is used as a technique to inspire you to follow my teachings, it is perfectly alright. When you create a gap between you and me, rest assured that you are just hanging me on the cross.

Trust even if you are exploited. The very title will make us wonder if it can be practiced in our life. It sounds too impractical. All sorts of questions arise in our minds, 'How can we lead a normal life on this planet? How can we protect ourselves? What is he teaching us?'

Let us understand what I mean by this statement. Let us go into the circuit of trust. We have consciousness in our being. Even if we don't accept Existence or God (because there is no proof), can we deny that we exist? Someone once came and asked me if he could attend the *Ananda Spurana Program* (ASP) and wanted to know what the requisite qualifications were. I asked him, 'Are you alive?' When he replied with a surprised 'yes', I assured him that it was the only qualification anybody needed. Every one of us has consciousness working in our system. If we can understand how it works at different levels and how it expresses itself, then we will understand what I mean by trust.

When consciousness expresses itself through the head, logic or intellect, our intellect becomes intelligence. What is the difference between intellect and intelligence? Intellect is always prejudiced. Intelligence is always fresh. When we pass judgment and collect evidence to support our decision, it is the intellect. When we first collect the evidence and then pass the judgment, it is intelligence. 99% of us make the judgment before we collect the arguments to support it.

All we have to do is just look at our life and see how our mind works. How do we act in our daily life? 99% of the time, our judgment is ready. For example, your son comes home late by a few hours. You make a judgment about him. You are not going to accept any of his explanations. It can't shake your judgment. On the contrary, you will only try to pick the arguments to support your decision. After that incident, whatever he does, you will always be biased by your previous judgment. Similarly, after living with your wife for a few months, you will create a concept about her. Then, no matter what she does, you pick up only those arguments that are necessary to support your judgment.

Recently, a man came to meet me and asked me to bless him for his divorce. In India, a master is not only a spiritual person; he is also a marriage-broker, stock-broker, financier, counselor, psychiatrist and a doctor! Of course, masters are supposed to do these things. Whatever decisions are advised by an enlightened person are always for one's good. Compassion and responsibility of the world descends on him. I asked this man to tell me the real problem before I gave my advice.

I always try to patch up the differences between people. One should have a very strong case before one takes such a drastic step. He replied, 'One morning, when my wife brought me coffee in bed, she spilt the hot coffee on me. The fight started from there.' He then went down memory lane to dig up all his arguments against his wife. Some communities in India have a custom at the time of marriage where the bride and groom try to grab a ring which is placed in a bowl of water. This custom is done more for fun, to act as an ice-breaker for the newly married couple. Whoever succeeds in grabbing the ring, gets to keep it. The man exclaimed, 'Right from that time, she spelled trouble for me. She scratched my hand.' See his mentality. He has forgotten how she used to bring him coffee in bed everyday; he has no gratitude for that. Instead, he blames her for spilling coffee on him once. We forget all the arguments which go against our judgment and pick up only those that support our judgment. If you scan your life and see how many times you do this, you will understand what I am saying.

Most of the time, if it is our emotion, we say it is love. If it is someone else's, we call it lust. For example, if we are angry, we say we are getting angry for the good of the other person. But we condemn others if they do the same thing to us. We say that the other person is egoistic. People come and boast about their deeds to me but they also quickly add that they are only informing me and not boasting. When other people do the same it is interpreted as ego but when we say the same thing, it is information. We have different arguments for others and for ourselves.

The prejudiced concept (collecting arguments for the sake of the judgment) will not allow us to live our life in an intelligent way. Whenever our consciousness touches the intellect, it becomes intelligence. Instead of living for the judgment, we start living for clarity. Right now, all our energy is spent on supporting our judgments.

We are carrying a 20-feet cut-out (a bill board) of ourselves all the time. Our cut-out is nothing but our judgments and our prejudices.

All our energy is spent on carrying the cut-out. If we have a big cut-out in front of us, how can we see the world? How can we see reality? Has anybody seen any strikes (protests) in India? (There is no need to see hell if you have!). These people can't see anything in the front. They are just guided. Similarly, when you live with prejudice and judgments, you will not see the world as it is. You will not see reality. When we carry these judgments, we can never forgive others or ourselves.

Forgiving others and forgiving ourselves is one and the same. Jesus says, 'Love thy neighbor as you love yourself.' Unfortunately we don't even love ourselves. Then how can we love others? When we torture others with our judgments and prejudices, we torture ourselves too. We use the same sword to kill others and to commit suicide. It is the same mind which deals with others as well as ourselves. When we try to poison others, there will be a deep sense of guilt in us because it is the same mind which is working. We use strong words when we are angry and once the anger dies down, the same sharpness which we expressed is turned inwards to create a deep guilt. The height of the anger and the depth of the guilt are equal. If the height increases, the depth increases as well.

Whenever we try to live for our judgments, our ego, our decisions, we make our lives as well as others' lives miserable. Most of the time, the miseries we face in our lives are not created by others. We may not even get any benefit from them. Just to prove our ego, we create them. Whenever we think that we are too big, we think that we are the judgment and all others are the arguments. When we realize that we are simple beings, we will start seeing the arguments clearly before passing judgment. We will start making decisions about our life as well as that concerning others in the right way.

An enlightened master, Suzuki, lived in Japan. When his master passed away, he started weeping profusely. One person asked him, 'You are an enlightened person; you shouldn't be crying at your master's death.' Suzuki replied, 'My master was the most extraordinary man on planet Earth.' The person asked him, 'What was so extraordinary about him?' Suzuki replied, 'I have never seen such an extraordinary person who thought he was the most ordinary man.'

In ordinary life, every average person thinks he is extraordinary. When one asks somebody to say something about his life, he will start off by saying 'Master, nobody in this world would have suffered like me. Even my enemies should not go through the same suffering. If I start talking about my life, you will not be able to bear it.' When one feels that they have undergone the maximum suffering, their ego feels good. Only when our enemy is big, do we feel big. When our enemy is small, we feel small.

That is why I say yellow journalism (writing about the personal lives of celebrities) is the worst thing a person can indulge in. Reading yellow journalism will spoil our minds. It is a direct visa to hell. These people target only the elite of the society. When they do so, they also feel elevated.

For the same reason, if our suffering is big, we feel good. Our ego is satisfied. We measure life by the amount we suffer. That is why we torture others as well as ourselves. Suzuki's master was extraordinary because he thought he was most ordinary, whereas in this world every other person thinks he is extraordinary. If one wants to check whether they are average or not, they can try this experiment. If one feels extraordinary, then quite clearly, one is average. If one feels ordinary, one is extraordinary. When people are depressed, they feel big and important. Whenever we have a judgment and then collect our arguments, we live intellectually. If we look deeply, we will realize that everybody thinks he is extraordinary.

A man who feels ordinary and believes in simplicity gives respect to everybody's arguments. He knows how to put himself in another's shoes. One's intelligence starts working then. When our consciousness reaches the intellect, whenever it works through the intellect, the intellect is transformed to intelligence. Whenever our intellect works through our heart and emotion, our love and passion get transformed to compassion. Whenever our emotion is expressed through the heart, our lust is transformed to love. Passion is transformed to compassion.

What is the difference between passion and compassion? When one advertises a product on a website, it reaches the entire world. Passion is localized but when we add the com, it becomes *com*passion and spreads throughout the world! Passion means focusing on one person. Compassion means focusing on the whole world. When everybody can access the passion.com, it becomes compassion.

A disciple once asked Buddha, 'Master, I have been listening to you for the last 30 years. You have been saying the same thing over these years. Why?' Buddha replied beautifully, 'Even after speaking for 30 years, only 3 or 4 people have heard what I have said.' That is why Buddha repeatedly said the same thing in different languages, different angles, different views and different versions so that at least a few people would be touched by one of these versions. Similarly, I also have been teaching the same thing from day one. If people listen with deep attention, they can understand that the message has been one and the same though I would have said it in many different ways.

When we don't pass judgment on others, we reach the state of acceptance; we reach the state of compassion. When intelligence happens, only then do we reach the stage of acceptance.

I read a survey of Bangalore in India which says, 'Only 17% of the population filed for divorce in 6 months. The remaining 83% don't have the courage.' Sometimes, acceptance also happens out of fear because we don't have the courage.

Acceptance is only the first step but not the final step. When we welcome other people and situations, compassion happens. *Beloved* means being loved; it is not about bodily love. If it is true love, we cannot love somebody and hate somebody else. Love can never be an act. The word 'love-making' is simply false. An act can only be lust. When real love happens, it flows. It flows for everybody. It is not restricted to one or two people. If we feel it for only one or two people, we can be sure that it is not true love. It can however be called selective amnesia!

For example, the relation between a mother-in-law and daughter-in-law, in most instances, is one of hate. The mother-in-law pretends that she is deaf but hears only what she wants to hear. I call this selective amnesia; remembering only what we want to remember. We forget other things. We can be sure that when we love somebody and hate somebody else, we do not know love. What we experience is simply different versions of lust. Lust does not only pertain to sex. Even a deep attachment to a son or daughter is a version of lust. When real love happens within us, our whole being flowers.

Some people come and tell me that out of love, they have given donations to temples and ashrams. They might have given donations but they also insist on having their entire family's names mentioned somewhere that everyone can see! A tube light may have the names of an entire family – 'Donated by Ramanathan, s/o Somanathan, wife Parvati in memory of Late Shri Shyamanathan on 20th December 1998. When one switches on the light, one can only see the black lines caused by the writing. Even if it is not written, they see to it that whenever they bring any guest to the temple, they become aware of the donation.

Never think of good deeds or attention to others as love. They are different versions of love. Freud says, 'Whatever you do, even writing with a pen, is a sexual act.' At first when I read it, I thought he was crazy, totally impractical. However, I then realized what he meant. What he meant was that they were all different versions of lust, not love.

Love is the flowering of our consciousness. Whenever our consciousness expresses itself through the heart, compassion happens; lust becomes love. The touch will become so vibrant, so soothing. I firmly believe that love is the greatest healing power on this planet. I tell my healers, 'If you can't spread love, you can never heal.'

When people come to meet me, I always stretch out my hands as soon as I see them. Many feel strange. They feel that spirituality means seriousness, being reserved, being unavailable. Here I am reaching out to people with my stretched hands. It doesn't match the picture of spirituality or the spiritual man. Spirituality is never associated with sharing or loving.

People from various backgrounds with various types of ailments visit our ashram to be healed by me; young people, old people, cancer patients, the disabled and even HIV patients. If a person has pain in their leg, I get up from my seat and bend down to touch their leg to heal them. I never differentiate between hands and feet. It is one body, the same body. An elderly, traditional and conservative *Swami* gave me some friendly advice about this practice. He said, 'You are a *Swami*. It is very unbecoming of a *Swami* to come down from his seat and touch someone's feet. It is against the tradition.' I replied very politely, 'The very seat on which I am sitting and the robe which I am wearing (saffron robes) mean compassion. I got this seat because of my compassion. I am not here because of the seat. I am here because of my state not because of my status.'

Spirituality means flowing. Whenever we don't flow, when we are not in the mood to stretch our hands out or to welcome people with hugs, we should stay in our rooms. Stay locked in it so that we don't pass on our negativity to the world. This is the advice given by Swami Vivekananda. Vivekananda said, 'If you are depressed, don't come out of your room. There is enough negativity in this world. Don't add to the existing negativity.'

Don't spread your negativity or depression. Spirituality means spreading love and compassion.

Whenever we serve out of compassion, we never feel that we have served somebody. We will always feel that we have been given an opportunity to serve others. Vivekananda said, 'The hand of the person who gives should be below while the person who accepts, his hand should be above.' In our case, the opposite happens. The giving hand is above and the receiving hand is below. We should be grateful to God that we have been given the opportunity to serve somebody.

That is why Vivekananda replaces the word *seva* (service) with *puja* (prayer). *Seva* puts one on a higher pedestal. In *puja*, you are offering, not serving. When compassion happens within our beings, we will offer, never serve.

When consciousness expresses itself through the heart, it is expressed as compassion. When it expresses itself through the being or self, it expresses as energy. When energy expresses itself through us, we will have tremendous trust in Existence.

Once I was questioned by a lady devotee, 'Master, however much I try to respect God, I am not able to do so. I only end up fighting with him. What should I do?' I told her, 'Don't worry. When you are fighting with him, it just proves that you trust him.'

So fighting with God is perfectly fine. Let me relate another incident; this happened in the ashram. One morning, a lady ashramite started fighting with me. When I asked her why she was doing so, she replied, 'When I worship you, I also have the right fight with you.' This is very true.

Have you heard the story of Sishupala from the Hindu epic, the *Puranas*? It is said that when Sishupala, an enemy of Krishna was killed, his soul entered the body of Krishna and merged with Him. Everyone was surprised as to how an enemy could be enlightened. Krishna explained that though Sishupala was trying to kill Him, he was constantly thinking of Him, constantly remembering Krishna and this was enough to make him enlightened. So fighting with God is perfectly okay if you can trust Him.

The devotion of most people does not have the trust. When our consciousness expresses itself through the being, it expresses itself as trust towards the whole of Existence. If the energy can move the sun, the moon and the earth, why can't it move our being? Why can't we trust Existence? Is our ego bigger than the sun, moon or the earth? Our life is much smaller and simpler than planet Earth. When the energy can move our planet, why can't it move us?

J. Krishnamurthy says, 'Trust always does good. Unfortunately, we don't have the patience to allow it to work in our lives. We should allow the seed to sprout, the flower to blossom. However, if we keep watching it, to check when it will flower, we act like security guards with a weapon in our hands; our very threat will not allow it to flower.'

Take the life of Buddha. He tried all possible meditation techniques and spiritual practices with the utmost sincerity to get enlightened. When nothing worked, he decided to relax and let go of everything, trusting Existence. That very moment, He got enlightened.

Even in my life, after going through rigorous spiritual practices, I decided to drop everything as enlightenment was not happening. That very moment, something happened in me and I experienced the ultimate experience. Only when we let go of everything, trusting Existence, miracles can happen in our lives.

A small story:

Lord Vishnu and Goddess Lakshmi were in a very relaxed mood and having a chat. Suddenly, Vishnu got up from His seat and ran a few yards, then took a u-turn and came back to take His seat. Lakshmi was perplexed and asked Him, 'Lord, why did you begin to run and then why did you return immediately?' Vishnu replied, 'I saw a man in the process of stoning one of my devotees. I ran to help him. But I saw my devotee picking up stones to retaliate. Then I decided that he did not need my help.'

Not from my intellectual knowledge, but from my experience, I am asking you to trust Existence. If you believe me, if you trust my words, when you trust Existence and relax from your tensions, headaches, worries and problems, be sure that you will be taken care of. Miracles will happen in your life. When you put your energy on trust totally, something happens in you. Alchemy starts taking place in you.

But we are continuously ready to defend. The truth is that we are fearful, and hence our defensive behaviour offends others. Any country increasing its army, claims that it is for defense purposes. Every army calls its army defensive. Then, who is really offending? Our very fear, our insecurity, makes us enter another's boundary offensively.

Whenever we trust, even if we live without comforts, I promise, you will live like God on this Earth. Sharada Devi opened a charitable hospital in Calcutta. There were two counters there; one for the poor where medicines were given free, and one for people who could afford to buy their medicine. One of the employees of the hospital complained to Sharada Devi, 'Mother, even the rich people are standing in the counter for the poor, and availing of free medicine. What should we do about this?' Sharada Devi replied, 'Don't bother. When a rich man stands in the line for the poor, be assured that he is also poor. Just give him the medicines. Even if he has money, he is a poor man.'

She makes a beautiful statement, 'If you live with trust, even if you are exploited, even if you lose your comforts of the outer world, you will live like a God on this planet Earth. You will float, never walk. You will become a divine person.'

In a Zen monastery, if a person is to be ordained as a monk, he has to pass a certain test. He has to live in a small room surrounded by grass on all four sides for a month. He has to walk in a particular line everyday whenever he leaves the hut. At the end of the month, if he has not created a path in the line that he walked, if the grass in that line has not died, he is eligible to become a monk.

This may be strange but it is true. Only when man walks on grass, it dies! It never happens with any other animal. I think not only plants, planets will also die if man walks on them; that is why he has not been allowed to walk on other planets! Since he is allowed to walk on planet Earth, we are in continuous danger. We have piled up atomic weapons which can destroy Earth a hundred times over. So if there is war, it is going to be one last war, not the next war.

Once I went on a safari, on an elephant ride in a forest in Tamil Nadu. There, you are taken on a particular path into the forest and brought back on another particular path. I noticed that where the mahout had walked, the grass had died but where the elephant had walked, the grass was alive. Strange but true! The elephant is so much heavier than man. Yet, where the elephant had walked, the grass was green and where man had walked, the grass was dead and a patch had been created. This is not because of physical weight but because of negativity.

We feel so insecure that we continuously defend ourselves; we continuously offend others. The defensive mechanism in us offends everybody. People who always say, 'I am innocent; people are using me, are taking me for granted,' are the ones who will always offend others by saying such things.

People who never defend themselves will never offend others. It is our mind, our being, which never trusts others and sends out negativity. When a cow eats grass, it will grow again but if a man even walks on it, the grass dies! That is why in Zen monasteries, whenever a man walks on the same path and a patch is not created, they accept him as a man who can be trusted, a man who can't hurt anybody, a man who is established in *ahimsa* (non-violence).

One more thing: if we defend ourselves because of our insecurities, we will not only offend others, but we will also miss the joy of living on this planet Earth. If we trust, even if we are exploited, how much will we lose? All that we possess is nothing more than a sand castle.

According to the Hindu epic, the *Puranas*, Vyasa lived the longest possible life a man could live. When someone asked him why he didn't build an ashram, he replied, 'After all, I am going to live for a few years. Why should I build a house? Why should I waste my time?' Even in our lives, if we analyze deeply, we will realize that most of our problems are nothing more than fantasies.

When we go to God, He is not going to ask us how much we possessed. He will ask us how we lived. Our wealth and relationships are not going to accompany us. But the way we lived our life will come with us.

A Zen *koan* goes, 'Children build sandcastles on the beach till the evening. When they leave for home, they break them without a care.' We build castles with costly things' but we take them so seriously. Children have intelligence, not seriousness.

So, there are two choices: we can live offending and defending continuously, where even if we have physical comfort, our being will have nothing more than a wound, or we can lead a totally relaxed life with utter freedom and complete trust in Existence. We can have physical, mental, emotional and psychological freedom – LIBERATION!

The moment we start living with trust, we are liberated; nothing hurts us anymore. If we live with trust, we even live our deaths. If we live without trust, we will be killed by the fear of death itself. Every moment, we will be dying. With trust, even in our death, we will be living.

Trust may or may not give us comfort, but we will have tremendous bliss. Without trust, we will have a deep wound. With trust, we will flower; we will have bliss.

From Subconsciousness to Superconsciousness

This is actually the subject that all the mystics, all the masters, all the saints, all the sages who walked on this planet spoke about. Whenever they spoke, it was only this one single subject.

Whatever may be the words they used, whatever may be the titles that they gave to these discourses...we may refer to them as the 'Sermon on the Mount', or as the *Bhagavad Gita* or the *Koran*, or as the *Zend Avesta*, or the *Guru Granth Sahib*; whatever be the name, all the words from all the masters are about this one subject: from subconsciousness to superconsciousness.

Anybody who shares their wisdom, anybody who is intelligent, anybody who speaks a few true words about spirituality, anybody who gives some intelligence, speaks only about this one subject - that is - the way to take one from the subconscious state to the superconscious state. Life solutions, that is solutions to the problems that we are facing in daily, or anything related to intelligence, is directly connected to this topic: from subconsciousness to superconsciousness.

Whenever our thoughts, our activities, or our mental set-up are in a subconscious state, we directly move towards suffering; we travel towards *mithya*, which means something that is ephemeral and unreal. The moment our words or our deeds are conscious, we travel towards superconsciousness, *nithya*, or the eternal, the real. All our growth can only be in this direction: from subconsciousness to superconsciousness. If we are moving in this direction, only then are we growing; otherwise we are merely getting aged, and growing old.

Getting old is not growing. *Anubhava* is not *anubhuti*. In Sanskrit we have two words – *anubhava* and *anubhuti*. *Anubhava* means just getting old, having experiences. *Anubhuti* means learning from those experiences. Let me illustrate this point by taking a simple example:

People first touch the burning butt of a cigarette and realize, 'Oh! The cigarette end burns!' Then they touch the fire of a match and realize, 'Oh! The match fire burns!' Then they touch the fire of the stove and say, 'Oh! This fire burns too!' One by one they touch the various types of fire. By the time they come to the conclusion that all types of fire burn, they would be so old that their own bodies would be ready for burning!

This is *anubhava* – where one learns from experience. But we don't have enough time to learn from experiences. We do not have enough time to commit all the mistakes and learn. The saying, 'Learn from your mistakes' is obsolete. I say, 'Learn from others' mistakes! We don't have time to commit all possible mistakes and learn. *Anubhava* is the path of subconsciousness.

The next is a beautiful word, *anubhuti*. This means learning straightaway from one mistake. It means the understanding gained through touching fire once, and immediately realizing that all fires burn - coming to a clear conclusion and understanding that all fires burn. *Anubhuti* is what I call the superconscious state, a state of pure consciousness.

Almost all religions, all rituals, all techniques, all meditations, are created only to drive man from subconsciousness to superconsciousness. Whatever we do, whether it is praying in the church, or offering *puja* in the temple, or doing *namaz* in the mosque, or any other ritual - all these were originally designed to drive man from subconsciousness to superconsciousness.

But the problem starts when we don't know the science. When we only do the act, when we act without knowing the science, we convert it into a ritual. When this happens, the process is made subconscious. *Anything done with knowledge, with wisdom, with awareness of the science of the whole action, becomes meditation.* When the science is lost and only the activity remains, it becomes nothing but a ritual. When the juice of wisdom is not there in the activity, it is just a ritual.

If the juice of spiritual wisdom is not there, we just remain religious nuts. When the juice of spiritual wisdom is added, we become spiritual fruits! So any ritual, any technique starts only as a technique to help us transcend subconsciousness and achieve superconsciousness.

But when we don't know the science behind the technique, we are likely to question the techniques: how does it work? Why should it help me? In what way is it going to add more energy, more clarity more intelligence to my life? When we don't know these facts, we inevitably reduce the whole thing to a sub conscious process.

When we know the science behind techniques, even just sitting can become a superconscious technique. Just sitting or simply inhaling and exhaling are more than enough to take us to the superconscious state. With intelligence and the right understanding, even a simple thing like inhaling and exhaling can put us into the superconscious state. This is what *vipassana* is all about. *Vipassana* is a wonderful meditation technique. I think the greatest gift given by the East to this planet is this *Vipassana* technique. *Vipassana* is the greatest gift given to planet Earth by Buddha. According to me, thousands and thousands of people have become enlightened just because of this one single technique. This technique is all about inhaling and exhaling consciously, that's all! If we know the science, if we are conscious, even simple inhaling and exhaling can lead us to superconsciousness. When we are not aware, when we don't know the science, even great and elaborate rituals can lead us only to subconsciousness.

Now, I will try to explain the science behind the technique: what is subconsciousness and what is superconsciousness; how we receive the information from the world and how the process of cognition happens in our system; how it becomes sub conscious and how it can be transformed into superconsciousness. I will explain based on Patanjali's (a great master who lived in ancient India) teachings. After I explain, we shall analyze the theory with questions and answers. The system of question and answers helps one to internalize. Actually, simple theory does not help us very much. When we analyze the theory with questions and answers, with discussion, it gets internalized in our systems.

So I shall now propose the simple theory:

Let us see how the mind works. Just look at this diagram here:

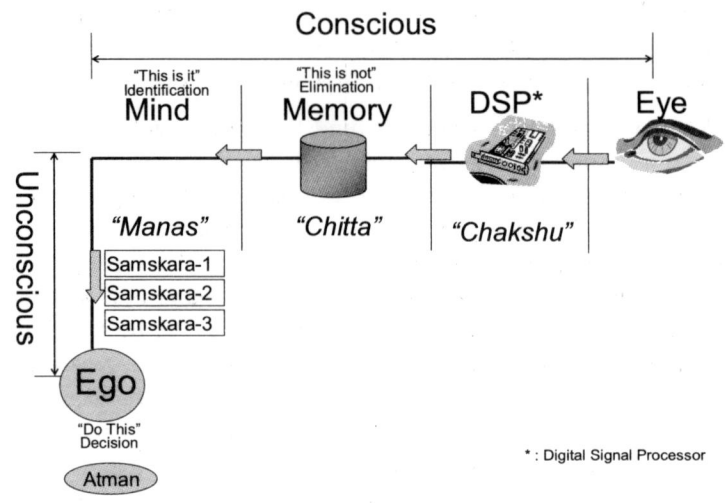

the eyes is processed; actually, not just information that enters through the eyes but information received through all fives senses - that is through the nose, ears, tongue, touch and the eyes. We will look at how information is processed through the eyes, as an example.

To begin with, we see something through our eyes. Let us take the example of, say, you seeing me. The moment you see me, there is an energy called *chakshu*, which converts the information into digital information. The nature of this energy is to digitize the information seen by the eye. If you want to process any information in the computer, you will have to digitalize it, is it not? Similarly, the energy called *chakshu* (*chakshu* in Sanskrit means, the energy that sees) converts this visual information, encodes into in the form of a file, and takes it to *chitta*, the memory bank. Here the work of analyzing the information begins. This is done through the process of elimination: It is 'not this', it is 'not this'. Identification does not occur here; only elimination occurs.

Then the file goes to the mind or *manas*. The mind does the job of identifying the file. It says, 'This is a cow; this a nurse etc.' The mind concludes, 'This is it.'

Next, the whole file takes a quantum leap to the ego, and your ego decides, based on your past experiences with what you are seeing, what your next action or decision will be. If you have past experiences with similar things that you are seeing, and they have been alright for you, if you think that it has helped you, you will decide to continue, or else you will think it is better to move on!

Now you are seeing me. The eye passes the information to the *chakshu*. The *chakshu* converts it to a digital signal. The memory then does all the elimination on the file – 'This is not…', 'This is not…' Then, the mind does the identification of the file – 'This is it'. Then the whole file takes a quantum leap to the ego. Here, you decide based on your past experiences, whether to sit here or leave the hall.

This process between the eye and the mind is logical and conscious. You are completely aware of this process. It happens with your awareness.

The quantum leap from the mind to the ego is mostly unconscious. That is the time when the actual decisions are made, and is mostly an unconscious process for you. It happens without your awareness. During this time, you simply decide illogically; you decide against your logical thought process. You make an illogical decision.

Why does this happen? Why do you decide unconsciously and regret it later?

The reason is, this unconscious zone is filled with negative memories and restlessness. All your past memories which we call *samskaras* in Sanskrit, are stored here. Without any logical connection between them. These memories or incidents are stored here.

What happens is, when the file takes a quantum leap to this zone, there is so much data stored, which causes so much restlessness in you, that the file does not even reach the ego properly for a decision. These stored engrams simply start playing upon the information received. They just impose themselves, and cause havoc in the decision making process.

As a result, the ego just makes a hasty decision purely at the instinct level, and passes the file back. It happens as an unconscious process.

For example, according to the data that you have collected, you know that smoking is injurious to your health; it is not good for your body or your mind. You hold on to this decision as long as you are in the conscious decision making stage of the process. Once the mind takes the leap to the ego, the files simply instruct you to smoke; you simply decide to smoke! The conscious process says, 'No, it is not good for my health.' But the unconscious process says... actually it doesn't even say... it just makes the decision and you execute it! It is a pure instinct-level decision.

As long as the unconscious is overloaded with negative memories and restlessness, it works at the instinct level, as we just saw. You simply decide instinctively, unconsciously. When you are at the instinct level, you always end up regretting most of your decisions. You wonder, 'Why did I behave in that fashion? This is not me! How did I allow this to happen? How did I make that decision?' This happens because the unconscious is working at the instinct level. At this level, you just associate things without any logical connection, and jump to a conclusion unconsciously.

When you can be free from your memories and be empty and blissful in this unconscious zone, if you can be alive and fresh every moment without the burden of your past, without the burden of these stored memories, the energy of your being will express itself in its purest form. When this happens, we can say that your intelligence is at its peak, because energy IS Intelligence. When this happens, you make decisions out of an energy called intuition, where you simply *know* with tremendous clarity.

When you are at the intuitive level, you will make decisions from the energy of your intuition, from deep awareness and peace, from bliss!

One person came to me and asked me, 'Master, I have the habit of smoking. I am not able to drop it. Can you please help me?' I replied, 'Please start smoking consciously; that is enough.' I did not ask him to drop the habit. I just asked him to smoke with consciousness and awareness. 'Feel the cigarette, feel the touch, feel every puff, feel the smoke inside your body, feel what is happening inside your system. Experience it. See how your mind reacts to it, how you feel. Be aware; be conscious of the whole process.' I do not know how you will believe this, but the person came back to me on the fourth day and said, 'Master, I'm not able to smoke at all! What have you done to me?' I said, 'I have not done anything to you; it is not my presence that has changed you. It is your presence that has changed you!'

For your transformation, my presence is not necessary, your presence is enough!

Your presence is more than enough for your transformation; my presence is not necessary. If you understand this one statement, you will be liberated from gurus! That is the ultimate liberation. I tell you, liberation from gurus is the ultimate liberation! If you are able to understand this one technique: for transformation, my presence is not necessary, your presence is enough. Just infuse consciousness in the unconscious region. Infuse consciousness in every action, in every moment, and you will see that your entire life is transformed.

Actually, smoking is nothing but attempting to escape from some thoughts! So are all of our addictions! Analyze. Let us analyze all our addictions; analyze your addiction to coffee, tea, smoking, drinking, whatever it may be. At a particular time, we come upon a particular mental set-up; it may be depression, or a low mood, some mental set-up that we are not interested in facing. Either we feel that we do not have enough energy to face it, or we just don't want to face it. Immediately we drink something and escape from that mood! We just want to escape from that mood. We immediately turn to some escape route which may be tea, coffee, alcohol, smoking, eating, etc. Any addiction is nothing but an attempt to escape from the mental set-up for the time being, for those few moments. When we can't escape consciously, we choose unconscious methods, unconscious techniques.

A small analogy: a pig felt the stink from the sewers to be too much. In some parts of India we still have open drainage systems. The pig could not bear the smell. It put its nose into the filth to escape from it! In the same way, if we want to escape from suffering, we just make ourselves unconscious, and we think that we have escaped!

Drinking alcohol and other addictions are the same thing. When we are unable to consciously escape from a particular mental set-up, we take the help of some things from outside our system to make us unconscious; alcohol, smoking, drugs etc. Anything that makes us unconscious is dangerous for our decision making ability. We will not be able to make the right decision. Anything that makes us unconscious will naturally lead us to dullness. We will be abusing our body, our mind and our whole system. When we continuously use methods and techniques to reduce the awareness in the unconscious, it means putting oneself into unconsciousness. Naturally, we are traveling towards the path of suicide... slow suicide!

A small story in this connection:

Once a missionary was seen in a bar, going from one table to the other, talking to people, trying to convince them to give up drinking, and telling them how bad drinking was. One young person who was trying his best to avoid eye contact with the missionary, wanted to escape. To his horror, just then the missionary came and sat at his table in front of him and started advising him, 'Don't you feel what you are drinking is slow poison?' The youngster immediately replied, 'Yes I know. However since I am not in a hurry, I am taking this!'

One can drink, if one is not in a hurry to die! It is just slow suicide. It will make us dull and will bring down the intensity of our awareness; we will be traveling towards subconsciousness. Not just the habit of drinking - please understand, there are so many things that make us unconscious, that take us to subconsciousness. If we do something that is really not from our heart, but we do it anyway, it is out of desire or impulsiveness. Once again we are creating subconsciousness. Once again we help increase the depth of our subconsciousness. We get caught. We create a mental set-up that gives us more and more trouble.

Our whole life structure needs to be flooded with this single idea, with this single understanding. Once we do it, our lives will be simply transformed. If we are able to understand this one key *sutra* (aphorism), one *mantra*: infusing awareness into our unconscious zone, infusing awareness into the area where we make decisions - it is enough. If we can infuse awareness into the unconscious zone, our whole life will be transformed from that very moment. Transformation does not mean years, months, or even weeks. It is just a conscious choice, a simple decision: from today, I decide to transform my life.

If we are in the subconscious level, the moment we choose, we will move to a conscious level. If we are at a conscious level, the moment we choose, we will move to the level of the superconscious.

This is the ultimate technique, not only for spiritual progress, even to live life happily; this is the master key. Anybody, not only spiritual masters, anybody who is on this planet Earth, any intelligent man, any person with wisdom who happened on this planet Earth, if we see his teachings, if we read his words either directly or indirectly, he will be saying the same thing: *infuse consciousness into your decision-making zone.* Infusing awareness into the unconscious zone is the ultimate teaching. Neither can anything more be said, nor anything be removed from this teaching. All meditation, all spirituality, all techniques, are nothing but this one sentence: infusing awareness into our unconscious zone. That is the mysterious zone in which our decisions are made. If we can infuse a little bit of awareness, that is enough; we are already spiritual. We are becoming Buddha.

Now, what is the way? We all know that infusing awareness into our unconscious zones is necessary. How do we do it? Understand these three simple things: *whatever way your body moves, try to be inside your boundary.* Wherever you are sitting or standing, try to be inside your boundary. Just be inside your body. Let us look at your life. If you are in your house, early in the morning, you will be worrying about your office. If you are sitting in the office, you will be bothering about the evening to be spent at the beach. If you are sitting on the beach, again you will be worrying when you would be back at the house! Only one thing is sure – if your body is here, you are not here! That has become a mental set-up. So understand this first key: just be where you are. *If you are here, please be here! That is the first key.*

Next thing, *infuse awareness into your inhaling and exhaling as much as possible.* Whenever you are sitting, relaxing, watching television, playing, reading the paper, or driving, whatever you may be doing – one thing is sure, you are certainly breathing. Just bring in some awareness into your breathing. *Whenever you remember, try to infuse some awareness into your inhaling and exhaling. This is the second key.*

Third thing: *bring awareness into the words that you use with yourself.* We are continuously using words with ourselves: what I call a monologue. *Try to bring a little bit of awareness into your monologue.*

So, live inside your boundary; bring awareness into your breathing, bring awareness into your monologue. Here (pointing to the edge of the body) ends your body, and here (pointing to the air next to the body) the universe starts. Please live inside your boundary. If you can live inside your boundary, you will be liberated.

Please understand that life is a paradox. If you live inside your boundary, you will be liberated from boundary consciousness! The moment we start living inside our boundary, we are *jeevan mukta*. *Jeevan mukta* in Sanskrit means a person who is liberated while still alive. A person who has achieved spiritual freedom while still living in the body is called *jeevan mukta* in Sanskrit. Liberation does not mean achieving any special powers. Of course, we will have them once liberated. A liberated person is one who lives inside his boundary. If we live inside our boundary and start infusing a little bit of awareness into our inhaling and exhaling, and whenever we remember, bring awareness into our monologue, our inner chattering, we can never create guilt. Be careful not to create guilt. If you forget for a few moments, do not bother. If you create guilt, again you will be creating conflict within. Don't create conflict between the conscious and the unconscious. Don't create guilt. Whenever you remember, just infuse awareness into your inner chattering, to your inhaling and exhaling and to your body language. Just be aware, be conscious of your body language, how you are holding yourself, how your body is moving, how you are living inside your being, and just *be inside your boundary*.

These three simple keys can completely liberate one from subconsciousness. It can completely transport us from subconsciousness to superconsciousness.

Now, as stated earlier, I shall spend some time with your questions. Any question or discussion are welcome. If you are not able to accept anything of what I have said, you are welcome to open the subject, because whatever I said, will only be at the mind level. Unless you analyze with doubts, and questions and answers, you will not internalize it.

Is there a way to recognize a person who is superconscious?

A person who is superconscious will be serenely blissful. One more thing, the question itself will disappear. I tell you, if you go and sit in front of a person who is superconscious, the question itself will disappear. Try your best to doubt him; you will find that there is no root for your doubt! The root of doubt is logic. That will slowly start slipping. Without you being even aware, the pillars that hold your logic will slowly fall.

People ask me, 'Master, should I accept you as a guru?' I tell them, 'Never commit that mistake.' Me becoming your guru will happen on its own, unconsciously. You will not be able to forget me. If I am in your thoughts, in your dreams, in your sleep, then I am your guru. If that has not happened, just forget me and carry on with your life. So, if you are sitting in the presence of a superconscious being, this question itself will slowly start melting. Try your best to doubt, 'I don't think he is superconscious. Let us see...'

Try your best to create more and more doubts. The doubts will just wither away. The doubts will not stand. That is the only technique; nothing else can be done. You will be just beyond your mind, beyond your logic, beyond your doubt. The conclusion will happen inside your system. Then you can decide that the person is superconscious. There is no other technique, no other scale, and no other invented machines to find out if a person is superconscious.

Master, what about pain? Is it a mental problem? Can it be healed?

It is nothing but too much unawareness in the unconscious.

I shall give you a simple technique which I have spoken about in my discourse entitled 'Pain to Bliss'. The technique shows you how to infuse awareness into the places where you have pain - physical or emotional. Both can be healed when you infuse awareness. For example, let us say you have knee pain. Just relax, and start searching in the zone where you have pain. Naturally, around the knee area you will feel the pain. Now, drop the word 'pain'. If you see your inner chattering, you will continuously be repeating the word 'pain' again and again, without your awareness. Be a little aware and drop that word. Drop the word and see what is happening in that area.

Just as when a small child sees something new, how would it look at it? It sees it with all curiosity, with all excitement, is it not? In the same way, look at the area where you have the pain, with all curiosity, without labeling it as 'pain'. First thing, drop the word 'pain'. Do not use it. Secondly, just see what is happening there. You will see that some new feeling is there. What is that new feeling? Just see. And slowly you will see that the area in which you felt the pain, instead of the whole knee, the area of pain slowly starts shrinking. And instead of a small patch, it reduces to one point. Suddenly you will see that the whole pain disappears!

Understand: I am not proposing a theory. I have worked with at least ten thousand people using this technique. It works. I have worked with cancer patients; I have worked with acute arthritis, rheumatism, people who have got pain all over the body. Even with such patients, I worked with this technique. It works miracles. And apart from me working, many of our disciple doctors, they too have worked with this technique and they vouch for this technique. They have given testimonials for this technique, a simple technique wherein you infuse awareness in your boundary and inner chattering. When you infuse awareness in your inner chattering, the word pain can be dropped. You will not be repeating it sub consciously, intensely and continuously. You will first drop the word 'pain'.

Next thing: infuse awareness into your boundary; live inside your boundary. Infuse awareness to the area where you have pain. And the third thing, you can do this also, infusing your awareness into your inhaling and exhaling at the time of meditation. If you can do these three things, miracles can happen. People come out of physical pain and suffering.

Now I shall give you small tips about emotional pain.

All types of emotional pain are nothing but your inner chatter done without awareness.

Your monologue without awareness is the thing that leads to all emotional pain. If you can infuse some awareness and constantly edit your inner chattering, censor your inner chattering, you will release your emotional pain. For example, if an entire movie is released as it is from the studio, without editing, will anybody see it? After the shoot is over, if the entire film is just released without editing, what would happen? We are doing the very same thing in our lives. Whatever happens, we don't put enough time, awareness, consciousness and energy to do the editing process. That is why our life is a mess, just like a movie that has been released without editing.

If we start living without editing our inner chatter, we will make a mess of our whole life. So just infuse a little awareness whenever you are in emotional pain or psychological pain. Sit with yourself and look at your inner chattering. You will see that simple awareness itself is the cure.

A small story:

Once a great king went to Buddha and sat in front of him. The king was constantly shaking his legs, unconsciously. Buddha suddenly started staring at the king's legs. The moment Buddha's gaze fell on the king's legs, the king stopped the shaking. Automatically the king stopped the shaking! The king asked, 'Oh Buddha, how can I stop my mind?' Buddha replied, 'The same technique!'

The moment you become aware, you stop. The shaking of the legs stopped the moment he became aware of it. In the same way, the moment you become aware of your mind, it stops! The moment you become aware of your emotional pain - your psychological suffering, you get the release from it. All you need is to infuse awareness. As long as you are unaware, you are in the subconscious level, and you will have physical and psychological pains. The moment you infuse awareness, both physical and psychological pains just disappear, dissolve. You are not even solving them, you are just 'dis-solving' the pain.

One request: before trying these techniques, please don't decide that they will not work! This is my simple request. You see, when you come here, I don't demand faith. I don't ask you to believe in me. I don't ask for faith as a pre-requisite. But one thing: do not have negative faith. Neither have faith nor doubt. Just have simple curiosity to try, like a scientist. The real spirit of Science is trying to analyze, trying to work, trying to explore. If any hypothesis is proposed, they will explore. The curiosity or the capacity or the energy to explore, is what I need when you work with these techniques. Spirituality also needs the same spirit. A real scientist will always be curious and enthusiastic, to explore. Please have that much energy for these techniques too. Have the courage to explore. Then you will see that miracles will happen in your life. You will be simply transformed. When you listen to the techniques, they appear so simple. One may be tempted to think, 'No! This is too simple to work! All this will not work.' Or, if you feel it is too complicated, then naturally you will think, 'Oh! It is so complicated. It will not work!' In both instances, you arrive at a conclusion before you practice even once. Please don't do this.

Master, I am doing some mantra *from (so and so master). Lots of thoughts are coming.*

Any technique that you have received from a master, you should ask the advice or suggestions also from the same master, because he or she wants you to grow in a particular way and that is why they have given you some particular technique. If I now give some suggestion, there is a possibility of you getting disturbed. Suggestions or advice should be given only by the person who gave you the technique. It is like this: only the Ford Company can release spare parts for Ford cars! Only the person who launched the product can give the spare parts also. Only he will know the repair and maintenance methods! In this same way, she has given you the technique. Now only she can give the solution. And one more thing: you must follow only her solution. I request you to not follow my solutions, because my solutions are given to the people who are practicing *my* techniques.

During the discourse, you used two words, 'consciousness' and 'spirit'. What is the difference, and how does one know which is which?

When you are working, it is called consciousness and when you have achieved, it is called spirit, that's all. When you are working, that is when you are trying to infuse consciousness. The time when you work is called consciousness. When you have achieved, it is called spirit.

Let me give you this small example: consciousness is like 18 carat gold, while spirit is like 24 carat gold. If you don't have any doubts, you can be sure you have achieved the spirit. The work is over. If you have doubts and you are still working, it is consciousness. Consciousness is the path and spirit is the realization. In a way, you can say that the superconscious is spirit. Consciousness is your moving on the path.

Master, when I start doing vipassana *meditation, I tend to fall into depression, or some other emotions become strong. What is the reason? How can I overcome this?*

This is a nice question. Actually if you do *vipassana*, when you are in a state where you have suppressed your emotions, you will have this feeling. Your suppression, depression, everything will come up. The best way is, before doing the technique, start doing some catharsis. Do some loud *glossololia* which we call 'manipuraka meditation' in our Life Bliss Programs. **Glossololia** means, shouting in a language that you don't know. For five minutes, just start screaming. You may feel funny, odd. But when you do it you will understand; all your suppressed emotions will be cleansed. I always have this technique in my meditation camps. This type of catharsis meditation is a must in our meditation camps. Throw away whatever you have. Watch how once all the garbage is taken out, meditation just happens to you!

I will not force sanity upon you. Once the insanity is pulled out, sanity happens to you automatically. Sanity just blossoms in you. So before doing the *vipassana* technique, for about five or ten minutes, you can just blabber, or scream, or just make loud noises. Do something nonsensical and intense like this. You will see that your mind and body then easily settle into the meditative mood without falling into depression, because you have vomited everything out.

Master, the first time I heard your discourse, I felt shy to ask questions...

(*interrupts*) Actually, I always tell people, never feel shy to ask questions. The problem is that if you ask, you think you will look like a fool, as everyone will be looking at you. If you ask, no doubt you may look like a fool, but if you don't ask, you *will remain* a fool! Whether it is better to look like a fool, or remain a fool is your decision!

(*continues*): *This time, so many things you have explained I have never heard before...*

(*interrupts again*) Actually this is the Science of the whole thing. This is the Science based on which meditation techniques themselves are created. This is the master key for all the meditation techniques. Meditation techniques themselves are master keys. This is the master key of the master keys!

(Continues): I did notice a difference in me as compared to last time. My actions have changed; I am more aware. Earlier I was hyper. Now I think I am in the medium level. Maybe I will be much better by the time you come here next time. Maybe I will be a different human being!

The conscious decision that, 'I will be a different person by the time I meet you next time', is more than enough for the shift, for the transformation to happen. We don't respect the power of our conscious decisions. Actually, I don't think we respect ourselves at all in the first place! Then where is the question of respecting the conscious decision? We don't respect ourselves as an entity, which is why others also don't think of us as an entity. This is the basic trouble. If you think your conscious decisions are powerful, people will just follow you.

People come and ask me, 'Master, how do I impress others? How can I influence people?' I tell them, 'First influence yourself! Integrate yourself. Believe that you can influence yourself and others.' The moment you influence yourself, you integrate yourself; you become such a power, such an energy source, that people can't resist you; they will just follow you. Anybody whose consciousness has become 'a leader' will just start leading. Whatever profession you may be in, wherever you are, whether you are in business, or in a job, or you are a doctor, lawyer or whatever, if your consciousness is to lead, you will lead irrespective of anything else. If your consciousness is 'to follow', even if you are in the CEO chair, you will be following somebody, imitating somebody. 'Leader' or 'follower' is based on consciousness. It is based on the state of your mind, not the status of your chair. 'Leader' is a state, not a status. Please be very clear: people who have achieved the status without achieving the state can never stay in the status. Even if you are in the status without being in the state, you will not be able to enjoy it. If you are in the state, the status will just follow you. Even if you don't have the status, you will be enjoying your life.

So it is necessary to achieve the state rather than the status. Status will just follow you, if you are in the state.

You mentioned Patanjali. According to Patanjali, there are eight sutras *for enlightenment, starting with* yama, niyama *(observance of moral and social codes) etc. One among the eight is meditation. Before reaching samadhi (realization), you advocate meditation. However, can we directly enter into the zone of dhyana (meditation) without following the initial yama, niyama and other steps?*

This is a wonderful question. You see: this system was created for human beings who lived on this planet 2000 years ago. For them *yama, niyama,* etc was natural. The depth of fantasy was less. So *brahmacharya* (observance of reality) was possible. The need to tell a lie, was not there, so *satya* (truth) was possible. Since enough of protection was available, *ahimsa* (non-violence) was naturally possible. For the society of those days, all those things were possible. Even now it is possible, I don't deny it, but only after having the experience of meditation. Today's human mind is so complex. All these things are too much for it.

If you start working without having the experience of meditation, just in the way of *yama* and *niyama*, you will only be creating conflicts within yourself. You will only be creating guilt within yourself. Just try *yama* and *niyama*. I don't have to say. You will know for yourself what the experience is. I have always seen people coming and saying, 'Yes master, we have a little problem.' They come and stand before me and scratch their heads. Why? Even to practice *yama* and *niyama*, you need a certain amount of integrity and energy, certain awareness of the unconscious, which is not there in the modern man today. In the modern man, even that much awareness of unconscious is not there. Even to follow what your intelligence says, you need an awareness of the unconscious.

In this modern society, man has become schizophrenic. There is no person who can be termed a 'normal' man. The normal level itself has become abnormal. Or rather, the abnormal level has become normal! This is what is referred to as 'border-line' cases in medical language. People almost look normal. They walk, talk, etc almost normally. But once you go close, you're gone! That is why they say, before getting married, it is better to live with that person for at least 6 months! You will come to know whether he is a border-line case, or whether he's alright!

The abnormal level has become the normal level. So we need to do some meditation immediately, infusing awareness, so that we can become 'man' again. Then we can start practicing the *yama, niyama, asana, pranayama, pratyahara, dharana, dhyana,* and *samadhi.* There are seven steps. The eighth is not a step; it is an achievement. The steps are seven. But first you have to become 'man'. For that itself you need to increase your awareness.

Master, under your guidance I have come from Pre-school level to Middle school level. Now I want to go to High School level with your techniques.

The only technique to do is: increase the unconscious awareness; that's all. Actually, when you increase the unconscious awareness, you have started acquiring the real wealth. Goddess Lakshmi stands for wealth. Wealth here actually refers to increasing the unconscious awareness. The very word *Lakshmi* in Sanskrit means increasing the unconscious awareness. When you increase the unconscious awareness, with this same house you will feel more comfortable; with the same furniture, you feel more luxurious; with the same people, you feel blissful; with the same situations, you feel joyful. Actually *Lakshmi* is added when you increase the unconscious awareness. Of course, because of your right decision-making, wealth will also be added. The moment your unconscious awareness expands, your car becomes big, your bungalow becomes big, your life becomes big; everything becomes big - because of your decision making power, because of your clarity. Apart from that, your being, your *Lakshmitva* - the quality of being Lakshmi, the capacity to enjoy, the energy of the wealth consciousness, will just increase. Increasing the unconscious awareness is what I call 'creating affluence'.

Master, we have always been taught that ego is something bad, that we should try to get rid of the ego, but the way you explained, if there is sufficient unconscious awareness, the ego will let us make good decisions...

If there is sufficient unconscious awareness, the ego will disappear into the soul. Do you see this diagram? Under the ego, I have written *atman.* When the unconscious awareness is less, you are egoistic.

When the unconscious awareness is more, there is no ego. The ego just disappears. Only the *atman* shines. So it is all about unconscious awareness.

I pray to the ultimate divine energy, the consciousness, the eternal bliss which is in all your hearts, let you all understand these great truths and let you practice and experience the eternal bliss, *nithyananda*.

Fall In To Rise

Let me start with a small story of Buddha on this subject:
A popular and powerful Indian king wanted to see Buddha. So he went to Buddha accompanied by his ministers, representatives and citizens. He carried two things with him: a plate full of diamonds and jewelry and another full of flowers.
Buddha looked at his gifts: the diamonds and flowers. He commanded the king, 'Drop!' The King was shocked and dropped the flower plate. Again, Buddha said, 'Drop!' The king dropped the plate of diamonds at Buddha's feet.
Again, Buddha said, 'Drop!' Now the king was unable to understand what Buddha meant. He wondered, 'The first time Buddha asked me to drop the plate of flowers, I dropped it. The second time, Buddha asked me to drop the jewels, the diamonds, so I dropped them. Now again the Buddha is asking me to drop. I don't know what to drop!' He then asked Buddha, 'What should I drop?'
'Drop yourself. You will rise!'
Immediately, the next question arose in the king's mind. He asked, 'How should I drop myself?'

Quite commonly this is the very next question. The moment we bring in the question 'how', we have made the whole process complicated; we have complicated the entire process.

Let me explain what I mean by the word 'dropping', and how we are complicating it.

When I use the phrase 'drop yourself', there arises in us an idea of 'you', and the notion of 'dropping the you'. Whatever you think of as 'you', all your ideas about you, are based on your past experiences, your past decisions, your past understandings. Your idea of 'you' is only based on the past.

Our past experiences are wired into us, embedded into us. It is not only what the conscious mind recalls that comes back to influence us. Less than 2% of what we observe, what we experience is stored in our conscious mind. 98% is skipped by the conscious mind and goes straight away into our unconscious mind. We cannot recall these events at will. They choose to reveal themselves at their pleasure. It is as if you read a book of 100 pages, but can recall only 2 out of the 100 pages.

All the accumulated experiences of the past is what makes our present. Similarly all the accumulated experiences of the present is what determines our future. But somehow, we always ignore the present. We are rarely in the present. We constantly swing like a pendulum from our past to the future without staying in the present. Both the past and the future are unreal; only the present is real.

Our past is always in the past; it is always dead. That is why it is called the past. Yet, we always let this past affect us.

How do we do that?

In two ways:

- If we review our past decisions with our updated present intelligence, we will always create guilt in ourselves.
- Similarly, if we carry past references into our present decisions, we will duplicate the same mistakes from the past into the future.

Please understand these two things:

- If we review our past incidents or decisions using our *present* intelligence, we will create guilt in our being.
- If we make present decisions based on our past experiences, we will be replicating the same past into the future also; maybe in an updated fashion.

Even though we may not commit exactly the same mistakes, possibly by doing it a little differently, we will be moving in the same experiential level, in the same layer, in the same plane, not in a higher plane.

We do not have the intelligence to keep thinking of new ways to commit mistakes. Our mind falls into a groove, a track, a mind set, that forces it to do what it has always done. So we keep making the same mistakes as well.

However, instead of learning from our past experiences, learning from our mistakes, and rewiring our mind to do better the next time, what we invariably do is regret what we have done in the past and feel guilty. Feeling guilty does not solve our problems. To feel guilty is to be in sin. In fact that is the only sin. The hell that we talk about is not in another time and space. It is here with us when we feel guilty without doing anything to change our mindset. Hell is not geographical; it is psychological.

When we do something that turns out differently from what we expected, or against societal and religious codes, there may be problems and we feel guilty. We should understand that what we did was based on the wisdom that we had at that particular point in time and we should move on. There is no need to keep on thinking about these actions and feeling guilty, and doing nothing about changing our mind set.

The past is after all dead. Whatever you think of as 'you' is just dead. When I say 'drop', just disconnect from your past.

You can! You can disconnect!

Yet we always bring one more sentence into our mind, 'No, I have tried so many times, but I am unable to. How can I disconnect from the past?' When we say, 'I have tried so many times, I am not able to', again we have brought the past in. All our prior incidents also constitute part of the past. 'I tried', 'I am not able to', and 'I failed' are also past experiences. As long as we bring these in, how can we say that we have dropped the past? No! That's how you drag in more of the past.

When we bring the past again and again into our lives, into our present life, we live in the same mental set-up. In Sanskrit, we call it *samskara*. *Samskara* means 'mental set-up'- how we think, how we move, how we live. Our mental set-up is what can be called *samskara*.

We tend to create a particular *samskara*, a particular mental set-up, and again and again, we live only based on that.

At some point in our lives, we might have tried something, something which was impossible and naturally we would have failed. These failures get recorded in us in such a deep way, as such a deep impression, that repeatedly, only our failures come up to our mind, and we start thinking 'No, No, I cannot! I cannot drop the past! It is too big a job for me. I am not so courageous.' We bring these words again and again into our consciousness.

We forget one important thing though: any words which are brought repeatedly into our consciousness get power. Our consciousness gives power to everything. Anything which comes in front of us receives power, whether it is good or bad; it simply receives power. Any thought which appears in our being, starts getting empowered. Our consciousness is so powerful, so radiant, it gives energy, and it gives power to everything.

Any thought that is brought in front of our mind, in front of our consciousness, comes alive, just like a movie reel does in front of a projector.

Whatever slide is brought in front of a projector becomes reality. If a slide of a temple is put in a projector, one will see that temple in reality. If a slide of a church is put in a projector, one will see that church in reality. If a slide of an actor is put in a projector, one will see that actor in reality.

Any slide which we bring in front of the projector lamp becomes reality. Similarly, any word which we bring in front of our consciousness becomes reality; any word!

We can realize this clearly in the dream state. Imagine early morning, when you are just coming out of your sleep, when you are lying in bed, neither completely awake nor completely asleep, almost in a half-half state... at that time, if you just remember, or become aware of your dreams, you can see very clearly how the words coming into your mind are becoming visions, are becoming reality.

You might just have a word, an idea: 'I see my friend coming into my house', and you will see the whole thing happening in your dream. It will be words followed by experience. If you experience dreams early in the morning, you can understand what I say: words just appear in your mind and become a vision or experience.

Any word that comes into your mind gets power and becomes an experience.

I had a chance to live with a group of tribal villagers in Madhya Pradesh in central India. I myself saw them give birth to children without any pain: no pain, no assistance, no medicine, no attendant, no doctor, nothing! They gave birth to children without any fuss and they took care of themselves after that.

I was shocked. I asked them, 'How is this possible? Don't you experience any pain?' Their response was, 'Pain? What is pain?' The very idea of pain did not exist in their lives. Let me repeat this: the very idea of pain does not exist in their lives.

When that word or idea is not there in our minds, we don't suffer that idea. We suffer only that which we recall, remember or repeat again and again. Anything which is repeatedly recalled by us becomes our reality. It becomes a solid truth, the reality for our being.

If we keep thinking, 'I tried to drop the past. I am not able to', these words get repeated again and again inside our system. We decide we cannot drop the past; then we cannot drop; we just cannot achieve it.

The difficulty is, when we decide something solid, we collect arguments only to support that judgment. Whenever we decide something solid, whenever we have some judgment about ourselves, we collect arguments only to support that judgment. We don't think of anything else; we don't bother about anything else. All we do is, we create more and more incidents repeatedly; we create more and more arguments to support our judgment. Anything we believe, we make it stronger and we cling more to it. We never enter into reality. We create a big gap between reality and ourselves.

On the one side, all the spiritual mystics and masters declare again and again: whatever IS, is bliss! Whatever IS, is consciousness! Whatever IS, is energy! On the other side, the so-called normal people repeatedly say, 'Whatever is, is misery! Whatever is, is suffering! Whatever is, is troubling us.'

Where is the gap? Why does the same world look so beautiful for a Buddha, and so miserable for a *buddhu* (fool)?

It is a very deep mystery which we are unable to solve through our logic. Their country is the same, their situation in life is the same and their lifestyles are the same. Everything is the same! Except for their personalities, everything is the same. Yet, the ways in which they relate to the world are very different.

When we carry our past, we have a layer called the reactive mind that is unconscious, which decides for us. We do not make logical decisions. Please be very clear: a man who carries the past can never make any logical decisions.

Let me give you an example. Say you were disturbed years ago by somebody in a yellow dress and the incident created a deep imprint inside you. What happens is, you will recall it anytime you see somebody in a yellow dress. Unconsciously that memory will come up and you try to keep away from that person. When you meet someone in a yellow dress, you start with a negative judgment and if the person proves to be really genuine, then you open up. It takes you more effort and more energy to understand that person, and it is all because of this single experience in the past. This is what I mean when I say, 'Anybody who carries the past has a reactive mind.'

Let me give you another small example to understand whether you have a reactive mind or not. Say you are deep in thought and suddenly you recall something which you don't want to remember; some place, some person or some situation in which you were disturbed, in which you were abused. It comes up in your memory even though you don't want to remember it. Immediately you brush aside that thought. You say to yourself, 'Let me think of something else; let me think of something else.' You force yourself to change the course of your thinking. If you are doing this, be very clear, you have a reactive mind.

These memories which we don't want to recall or with which we are uncomfortable, are what I call energy clots; just like blood clots. When there is a blood clot, blood cannot flow freely. In the same way, these energy clots do not allow our thinking to flow freely. A person who has got more energy clots will always feel suffocated, stressed, and bound. On the other hand, take a person who doesn't have energy clots. His thinking will be free, his consciousness will be so free that he will never feel suffocated, stressed or bound.

It is the energy clots which decide whether we experience boundary-lessness, whether we experience expansion or whether we suffocate ourselves and continually get stressed. I have seen people feeling suffocated even when sitting on a beach. They will be sitting on a beach on their so-called vacation but they will not experience the boundary-less feeling; they will not experience the feeling of expansion.

I have also seen people who are living in small rooms their whole lives and are yet so free. There is a person in my native town who has been living inside a ten foot by ten foot room for the last thirty-five years. Thirty-five years! Nobody is binding him. He is actually considered an enlightened master and is worshipped as such. His name is Thinnai Swamigal; he is a disciple of Ramana Maharishi.

His is a beautiful story; let me narrate it:

He went to see Ramana Maharishi and asked, 'Bhagwan! How can I achieve any spiritual experience? How can I achieve enlightenment? Should I do a special type of worship? Should I use some type of mantra repetition? (a mantra is a sacred utterance, usually a syllable, the invocation of a God, or a portion of a scripture)? Should I chant some verses? Should I meditate? What should I do?'
Bhagwan casually said, 'Drop!' Just a casually uttered word, 'Drop!' This person was so sincere, he simply dropped. He really dropped. Something just dropped inside him. From that time until today, he is just sitting in a room nearby and living happily.
Nobody is binding him. Nobody is stopping him from going out. He just says, 'No, I am happy. I don't feel like it. If at all I feel like it, I will go.' Hundreds of people come there to see him. He is sitting there, radiating peace and bliss. He says, 'I feel totally expanded. I am boundary-less. Where can I go?'

There are people who are sitting inside a ten foot by ten foot room and feeling boundary-less consciousness; experiencing the universal consciousness. And there are people who are lying on a beach feeling suffocated and stressed! The experience of boundary-lessness has nothing to do with the outer world. It has to do with the number of energy clots that one has; the reactive mind that one has. When we drop the reactive mind, when we start to directly relate with Existence, our whole being is liberated.

Somebody went to a Zen master, and asked, 'Master, how can I achieve liberation?' The master just laughed, and said, 'Who has bound you? When did you get into bondage?' Immediately, the disciple just became enlightened.

When I say the word, 'Drop', whatever you understand according to your own Oxford Dictionary, just do that - that is enough! Whatever you understand by the word 'dropping', just do that. Whatever you think of as your being or whatever you think of as you, just drop that.

The difficulty is that we are afraid. Our past experiences are the only property that we have; our ideas of 'I' are the only asset that we have. These ideas are the only things that we have accumulated throughout our lives. How can we drop that? If we drop that, how do we live? What can we hold on to so that we may survive? All we have is our past life and past experiences. How can we be alive if we drop them?

I tell you: when we drop the past, don't think that the memory itself will disappear; our emotional attachment to that memory will disappear. Actually, when we drop the past, we will be able to live in the present in a much deeper way, in a much more intense way, in a much more beautiful way.

Again and again and again, if we read the teachings of all the great masters, it comes back to only one point: drop, or fall. Fall in, so that you can rise.

Notice an important point here. Instead of falling in, many a time, we fall outside towards the outer world. What I mean by this is that we fall for things which are in the outer world. Of course, whenever we fall towards the outer world, naturally we will make only that our reality. That will become a solid truth in our lives. Whatever we think of as truth, we will fall for that. Whatever we feel and fall for, we will make that our truth.

- If we think the outer world is truth, we fall for that. If we fall for the outer world, we make that our truth.

- When we fall in, fall for the inner world, we make the inner world our reality. When we make the inner world our reality, we fall more for the inner world.

So this is like a vicious circle: if we fall for the outer world, we make it our reality, and this leads us to fall more for the outer world. And if we fall for the inner world, we make that our reality and again this leads us to fall more for the inner world. Either way, the circle goes on.

Which way you want to travel is in your hands; this is what we are supposed to decide in life. We call this *pravritti* or *nivritti* in Sanskrit. Our choice is either towards the ephemeral or towards the eternal. It is our decision whether to travel towards *pravritti*, towards the ephemeral, or towards *nivritti*, towards the eternal.

When we drop the past, we simply travel towards the eternal. We travel towards the ultimate. We travel towards our being. And we just remember what we are, and what actually our being is.

Let me narrate a small story:

There was a king who ruled over his country. He had a son, who was a no-good fellow. The king was very unhappy about the prince's attitude and lifestyle. He wanted his son to change his ways. He decided to teach his son a lesson. So he told his son, 'Leave this country! Go out and stay somewhere else for ten years. If you are able to maintain yourself for ten years, then I might take you back.'

So the prince was sent out of the country. He was the prince, so all he could do was sing, dance and enjoy himself. He didn't know much of anything else. So he moved around begging from house to house, door to door.

Ten years passed. The king said to himself, 'Now it is time to send people out to search for my son. We need to find out if he has managed to survive and what he is doing.' He sent his people out on the search. One of the ministers in the search party comes upon the prince begging by the roadside. The minister approached him, touched the beggar's feet and said, 'Sir! Do you remember us? You are the prince of our country. The king wants you to come back. The citizens want you to come back. Please come back.'

The moment the minister touched his feet, the prince's whole body language changed. He had been a beggar until that moment. The moment the minister touched his feet, he said, 'Oh! Is that so? Alright. Go, get my chariot!' The man's whole body language changed, beginning with his tone and extending all the way to his mental set-up. He climbed into the chariot and strode majestically into the palace.

His mental set-up was now completely different from what it had been when he was begging. He could never associate himself again with his past as a beggar. His lifestyle, his body language, his mentality, his thought process, everything was now new. It did not take much time for his mental set-up to change.

The prince didn't ask the minister, 'How can I change? How can I drop my past? How can I change my mental set-up?'

No!

In just a single moment, the whole cognitive shift happened!

The cognitive shift takes only a single moment, a single second. All we need to do is, believe that the kingdom of God, His heaven, is straightaway available to us, and open our eyes and start living. We tend to equate the kingdom of God with special angels, special choruses, a special group of people taking us to a special cloud, where all the saints are singing 'Hallelujah!' Just drop all these fantasies. This very land can become heaven. This very life can become heaven. This very life can become the kingdom of God.

All that we need to do is, instead of connecting all the negative incidents of our life and creating an idea about ourselves and the world, connect all the positive incidents of our life and create an idea about ourselves and the world; that's all. Nothing else needs to be done.

Be very clear: there are positive things in at least 50% of everyone's life. That is why we are still alive. If everything is completely negative, we can't even live. Your being here now, your being here to read this book is enough proof that at least 50% of your life is positive.

The difficulty is that we have developed our mental set-up such that we cannot survive without worries and negativity. Just scan your mental thinking. If you feel relaxed, open and empty some time, you start feeling uncomfortable. You start searching for some worries, something to think about, something to ponder over, something to contemplate. You cannot live in boundary-less consciousness.

You continuously feel that you need something, some material to chew on. That is the reason why you catch hold of some subject or the other, and start pondering. If you cannot find any subject, if you are not able to rehash any material, you start fearing, 'How long will life go on smoothly like this? I don't know when it will change. I don't know when bad things will start happening.'

We always start worrying about something else. We are habituated, trained to connect all the negative things and create an idea about ourselves and about the world. Please be very clear: we judge the world in exactly the same way we judge ourselves. We never believe that others are speaking the truth, because *we* never speak the truth.

You can see that we always think, 'When I am like this, naturally the other person will also be the same. When I live like this, naturally he will also live like this.' We judge everybody else in the same manner that we judge ourselves.

The Bible says, 'God created man in his own mould.' I tell you one more thing: man creates the world in his own mould. Whatever you think of as 'You', you create the world in the same mould. You project the same world. Whatever idea you create about yourself, that idea also plays a major role about your idea of the world. It is you who creates and projects; it is you who experiences.

The difficulty is, we never leave any separation between ourselves and our thinking system. We associate too much, get too caught up with our thinking system; we never begin to suspect it. We never suspect our thinking system and our perceptions. We never doubt it. We doubt everybody else, but never ourselves.

Before satisfying any desire, our mind says something. Once we achieve that desire, our mind says the exactly opposite thing. Even though this is repeatedly our experience, we never suspect our mind. We never doubt our mind.

Before achieving it, we might think about an object in a specific way. Before achieving a goal, even a mustard seed looks like a mountain. We desire the object; it is as if we cannot live without it. I was browsing the 'Sky Mall' in-flight magazine on my flight here. They word the advertisements for products in such a wonderful way, that you feel that those products are basic needs. You feel as if you cannot live without those products!

Before achieving a goal, even a mustard seed looks like a mountain. Once we have achieved it, even a mountain begins to look like a mustard seed. Again and again, the mind cheats us. We run, run, run, run, run to achieve something. The moment we achieve it, we find a feeling of emptiness coming up inside us.

Still, we never suspect our minds. We doubt and suspect everything else except our idea about ourselves and our idea about the world. This is what needs to be doubted; this is what needs to be suspected. The moment we start doubting our idea about ourselves and our idea about the world, we drop; we just drop. This doubt is more than enough; the very doubt is enough to give us the courage to drop. As long as we don't doubt our understanding, we keep going on and on.

I was watching a beautiful movie the other day, 'What the Bleep Do We Know.' It is a wonderful movie! The filmmakers have done a great service to the world by making that movie.

One of the people in the movie asks a beautiful question: our dreams and this world are both seen by our brain in the same way, in an equal fashion. Then how can we say that one is reality and the other is a dream? How can we claim that one of this is reality and the other is a dream conjured by the mind?

They create basic doubts which are supposed to be created in every individual, in every human being. The moment we enter into this doubt, we drop. When we drop, we really rise.

When you fall in, you rise. You rise to the ultimate experience, the ultimate consciousness, which we call Divine, God, Universal Intelligence, or Cosmic Energy. So I pray to that ultimate energy, the cosmic energy: let us all fall into it, and become the divine energy, that eternal bliss, *nithyananda*.

QUESTIONS & ANSWERS

Can you talk a little bit about the issue of speed? The world in many contexts seems to be moving faster and faster and faster. What impact does this have on our consciousness and our ability to drop?

The faster the world moves, the more difficult it is to drop. The faster the world moves, the more information we get. We are processing much more information and this also adds stress. Amidst all this processing, we forget to question the basics.

One important thing to note is, when everybody is engaged in so much work, we forget to question the whole system. There is so much to get done, to be accomplished, that we have no time to question the basic stuff underlying the system.

That is why in India, the first thing they do in their traditional education system is, raise basic doubts. Until the age of twenty five, nobody can take up any job.

Each person will have to raise basic doubts and live with them; and question again and again; search. Only when they achieve the balance of discovering the answer unto themselves, into their being, only then are they allowed to enter into life: whether into marriage, making money, or anything else.

Until the age of twenty five, it is called the period of *brahmacharya*. This period means studying, living with Existence, living with doubts, searching within one.

Of course, the greater the speed of the world, the less possibility there is of dropping.

You can drop *out*, but not drop *in*.

Are there many phases to this dropping in? For example, you talked about one phase, this person who is living in a ten foot by ten foot room?

Yes, there are many phases. Just see what happens when you drop in.

What happens after you drop in is tremendous, totally different from what you might imagine it to be. But dropping in is only one thing; one aspect. Once you drop in, whatever happens when you rise, rises in thousands of ways - different for each person.

One person might go around the world and preach. Another might sing and dance, like the great enlightened lady Meera. Another might sit under a banyan tree like Buddha. Some may just walk around without clothing, like Mahavira. There are so many expressions after dropping in.

But the dropping in is common for everybody. After that, when you rise, you rise in many, many ways. Ramana Maharishi himself never sat inside a ten foot by ten foot room. He moved around within the whole city, although he never went outside the city. But his disciple has been sitting inside one room.

So each one to his own method of expression. Buddha was quiet and silent; peaceful. Krishna was singing and dancing. So, it is totally based on the individual's experience.

Things are speeding up so much that we cannot drop. In general, everything seems to be moving faster, so it almost seems like it is by design that we should not drop.

I think we must take a little time to doubt basic conclusions.

The other day I read a beautiful book, *The Final Theory*. If you have read that book, you might have been just as surprised as I was. Basic ideas about gravity - Newton's laws, Einstein's theories, everything is questioned; everything is questioned. I was shocked! How did we miss such basic questions about these theories?

When we accepted Newton's theories or Einstein's *Theory of Relativity*, everything fell in place. But from the book *Final Theory*, you can make out that there are so many basic scientific questions which have not been raised at all.

So before going further, we must raise some basic questions. We must take time to doubt basic ideas. We cannot put the responsibility on society saying, 'It is speeding up; it affects me in this way, so I cannot, etc.'

Of course, when we say that we cannot, we will go along with it, no problem there. But if at all we want the truth, the ultimate experience, if at all we are really in search of bliss, we must raise these questions.

See, there are two things that we are all searching for: some people are searching for status, some for the state. If one is looking for status, one can run with the speed. Status is different from state. If the state comes, status will follow. If status comes, we cannot be sure that the state will follow. So if we really want to achieve the state of bliss, we have to question the basic assumptions which we have made.

Master, what are the steps to drop? You just said, 'Drop.' How do we empower the mind to drop?

The first step is to drop this idea. The mind will then empower you!

But you will say, 'The mind is too difficult; I have tried this so many times; the mind never accepts.' All these are just ideas which you have given strength to. Just try to relax from these ideas.

Decide: for the next ten days, I will not repeat these ideas in my mind. I will not allow these words to come into my mind.

For just ten days, don't give any power or strength to words such as, 'It is very difficult to drop, master. You don't know. It is easier said than done. I have tried many times. It is very solid. The mind is very complicated.' Just don't give power to these words for ten days. For ten days, repeat 'No! The mind can be dropped. After all it is I who is thinking.'

To be sure, are you clear that nobody else is sitting inside you and thinking? Are you the one who is sitting and thinking? When you are sure that it is you who is sitting and thinking, why can't you change? It is you after all. It was you who created your world, your perceptions of weakness, word by word, sentence by sentence.

The moment the first word comes into your thoughts, just catch it. Why do you allow the whole sentence to come out? Then you go around crying, 'Oh! This is difficult! That is difficult! This is difficult!' The moment the first word comes out, catch it. Just say, 'Stop! For ten days I am packing you off on a holiday!' So just from today, for ten days, decide: for the next ten days, I will not give power to these words.

I tell you, after the tenth day, these thoughts will never come back. I tell you, in the last two years, I have met close to a quarter million people individually. And I have two thousand healers doing healing service in over one thousand centers in thirty three countries. With all my experience I tell you, I have seen at least ten thousand people like you who ask this question. Exactly the same question! All the ten thousand can drop. And there are many thousands who are successful. Just for ten days, not more than that. I am not asking you for anything more than that. Just for the next ten days decide: I will not repeat these words and give power to these words.

All these are just words, pure words. It is you who creates these self-contradicting words and gets into trouble. We go and face the corner of a room where the two walls meet and we cry, 'Oh! I am in a prison! I am in a prison! I am caught! I am caught!' We never turn and see the third side; we never turn and see that the room is actually wide open. We never take the time to turn around to another side and see that we are free; that we are liberated.

We are always binding ourselves with the 'second person' - 'you' and 'third person' - 'he'; we are always looking at the outer world or feel we are being looked at by others. We look at everything else other than ourselves, the 'I', the 'first person'. We never look into the 'first person' to see that we are liberated.

First of all, there is no 'first person'. We always see our face in the 'second person' and the 'third person'; and we think that we are bound by the way we are seen. Just turn around and look at yourself again. There is no 'first person'. When there is no 'first person', how can there be second or third persons? Neither are we bound nor do we need liberation.

All our fears, our worries, our feelings of separateness, are built on our idea of being the first person; our idea of 'I'; our idea of the 'first person'. The 'first person' himself doesn't exist. He is not there in the way we think. Please be very clear: in the way we think, he is not there. Just turn in and see! He is not there. Then why do you need to liberate yourself from the 'second person' and the 'third person'? There is no need.

But as long as we are hitting our head against the 'second person' and the 'third person', we will never be liberated. It's like we are hitting our head on the wall; we can never be liberated. The moment we turn in and see, the moment we fall in, we will see that there is no 'first person' and therefore there is no second or third persons either.

We are just fighting with our concepts. We are just fighting with our so-called fears; our self-created boundaries and anxieties. The fear of separateness is nothing but a concept. It is just based on, built on the concept that we are somebody. When we look, we will understand that we are not as we think.

I have been in constant physical pain for the past 5 years. Can you help?

I can help you in two ways.

The first is: try to drop that word 'pain' and start seeing the whole thing as a new experience. If you are feeling pain somewhere, just see what is happening in that area, like a child would look at something new, with curiosity. That is the first step.

Next, I will try to help you by healing after the class.

Both of these will help you.

This is a follow-up question to when you said that there are thousands of ways in which we can rise, after we fall in. Some people laugh, some stay quiet, etc. Is it possible for us to do the same things that we are doing every day?

Of course! You will do the same thing every day, but in a different way; a much better way, that's all.

Your energy will not be sucked in as it is currently by your psychological worrying. Right now, up to 80% of your inner chattering is taken up by unnecessary worrying.

Try this simple experiment. Speak whatever comes to your mind for ten minutes and record it. Whatever comes up, don't edit it, just record it as such. Then transcribe the tape; write it down. Read the page.

You will find that not even 10% of what you have written is directly related to your life, or is going to help you. Not even 10% of your thoughts will be directly related to your life. You will find that there are things simply going on in your mind. It is almost like running a lunatic asylum. Each sense is pulling the mind in different directions; there are so many different kinds of thoughts. You don't even realize this most of the time.

But when you drop the past, once you start living in the present, once you start experiencing consciousness, this waste of energy will not be there. You will not be drained so easily.

We are drained so easily because even to make a single decision, we have to move our file through ten thousand tables. Thousands and thousands of our energy clots have to say 'yes'. Only then will we be able to make a single decision. If the energy clots are removed, we will be able to make that same decision in a split second.

The other day in St.Louis, the doctor who has been researching my neurological system, was analyzing what happens in my brain at the time of meditation. He says that my right brain is very active; many times more active than the left brain. He said that the information in my brain will be processed so easily and so quickly. If the left brain takes minutes to process some information, the right brain takes only a fraction of a second to process that same information. He said, I would simply be making decisions without any worry.

He also says that the right brain is more related to global thinking and timeless zones. He said that I will be continuously experiencing the timeless awareness, which is the greatest freedom.

Time-bound awareness or space-bound awareness is what we call bondage. We call this, *banda* in Sanskrit. Timeless awareness and spaceless awareness is what I call *mukti* or enlightenment - liberation.

So all you need to do is to drop the past, and you will find that you will be able to do your job in a much better way, a much more creative way, a much more beautiful way, a much more spontaneous way and a much more responsible way.

This ability to make spontaneous decisions, is what I call responsibility. If you are able to make spontaneous decisions, you are responsible; you have responsibility; you become responsible not just to yourself in a selfish way but to all those around you. You will start radiating love and compassion. You will experience and spread eternal bliss, *nithyananda*.

Lust to Love: the Ultimate Alchemy

What is alchemy?

Alchemy is a process of transforming anything base to its higher form.

> When I was wandering in the Himalayas before enlightenment, once I met an old mystic - a naga baba who belonged to the spiritual sect of mystics who wore no clothes. I had been told that they are violent by nature. Many people who look at their wild faces and matted hair, feel scared to go anywhere near them. He was sitting on the banks of the sacred river Ganges. I went up to him and started talking to him. He was smoking ganja (marijuana). I watched him. He placed two copper coins inside his pipe and started smoking. When he had finished smoking, he emptied the pipe and two gold coins fell out! He sold the gold coins, bought more ganja and repeated the process of producing gold coins. He did this about 10 times in two days. I asked him to teach me meditation, as I did not want gold coins. He looked at me and gave me his pipe. I moved away as I had never liked the smell of tobacco since childhood. When he saw me move away, he put the pipe to his mouth and playfully blew smoke rings onto my face. For three days after that, I was in deep bliss.
> The process of changing a lower level metal such as copper or iron, into gold, is alchemy.
> I asked him how he did it. He replied to me in Tamil, my mother tongue! I had never told him about my background - who I was or where I was from. He said, angam pazhuthal thangam pazhukkum, which means, 'If your being is ripe, gold will ripen.'

When our being is ripe, we have the capacity to ripen anything. Great masters bring about radical transformation in people just by their presence, by the very quality of their being. Lust changes to love when your being is ripe; a base feeling transforms into the highest emotion you are capable of.

Someone asked Ramana, 'Give me the power of miracles.' Ramana said, 'You cannot even handle what power you have now; why do you ask for more?' The man asked, 'What power do I have?' Ramana said, 'You are a manager; you can hire people, dismiss people, do many other things. Are you handling these well now? If you were, you would not be stressed, you would already be at peace. What you need is intelligence, not power!'

Inner transformation is the ultimate alchemy that we need; not magical powers.

Miracles are foolish. There is no miracle that you need to put your effort into and perform. Miracles are happening every minute around you. Existence is causing miracles in everything around you every minute. People ask me repeatedly to perform miracles. It is so pointless to do it. If I start performing these so-called miracles, people will come only for the magic show, not for real transformation. I once clapped my hands and produced a Lakshmi deity. I told the group that it is just a sleight of hand. I cannot create objects, I can only teleport them. I moved the idol from my room to where my hand was. The principle is similar to how waves move between cell phones and transport voice. I converted the idol matter into energy, teleported it, and reconverted energy to matter, that's all. It is a Science.

If all cell phones except two were destroyed, the owners of the two cell phones will become Gods! When we do not understand the cause, we call an incident a miracle. Personal transformation is the ultimate miracle that we can get from a master. I had a disciple, a magician, who used to produce *vibhuti*, (sacred ash that Hindus wear on their forehead and body), from my feet. I told him, 'You are doing what I cannot do!'

People asked me, 'How do we know that you moved the deity from your room?' I produced a *mala* (chain) and told them to check the stock in the store room; one was missing!

So coming back to alchemy, the alchemy of converting copper to gold, comprises three processes: removing base components, adding some components and processing it so that a base metal gets converted to gold.

What is lust? We only know how to reproduce; we do not know lust. When animals come together, they experience pure lust. They enjoy themselves. On the other hand, our lust is taken from imagination, from movies, from books; it is not natural. From early years, we form ideas about how our 'would be' *should* be. This spoils the relationship. We relate to a person in our imagination, not the real person in front of us. The real husband or wife becomes a poor substitute to what is in our mind, our cerebral layer, which leaves us with a feeling of being cheated. Males feel they are deprived. Females feel exploited, used, disrespected. Our lust and sex are made impure with the dirt of imagination. We relate with them only mentally. In the *Shiva Sutras*, which is a set of verses delivered by Shiva to His consort, he says: in bed, you are four, not two – the husband and his fantasy woman, and the wife and her fantasy man.

In ancient times, at forty years of age, lust and sex left the householder, because they had enjoyed these in totality when they indulged. In the Hindu wedding ceremony, in the sacred *mantras* chanted in front of the fire, the wife says to the husband, 'Become my eleventh son' and the husband says to the wife, 'Become my eleventh daughter.' In the eleventh year of their marriage, their intimacy is so great that they become each other's child. There is a deep intimacy; there is a wonderful relationship. These words were not poems to read; they were living guidelines.

These days, marital relationships are a business, for security or material benefits. We may live in the same home, but not in a homely way. Remove the imagination and dreams from your lust; about both, your partner's body and yours. Many of us are ashamed of our bodies; we hate them. All body pains and chronic skin diseases arise out of low self-esteem and disrespect to one's own body. We would like to be someone else all the time. We would like to shape our body and dress like someone else. We stop staying in our boundary because of this. Whenever we hear our name, we think of our face, never our whole body, because we are not comfortable with our bodies. When we try to copy others, when we try to imitate and do not accept ourselves fully, we can at best be beautiful, but never graceful. Grace comes from within. For the next few days, look at your body after your bath with love; feel comfortable. Our body oozes bliss all the time. Yet we feel only the pain. If we are relaxed with our own body, our mind will not wander. When we are at home, our mind is in the office and when we are working we wish we were at a party. The main reason for this wandering is that we are not comfortable with our body.

Tulsidas, the poet says in his *Ramayana* about Sita, 'When Sita entered Janaka's court, all the *rishis* (sages) including Vasishta the great writer, and her own father, stood up to pay their respect to this young princess; such was her overwhelming grace.' In *Tantra* meditation, they touch their body first thing in the morning after they wake up. Every point in the body, they touch with deep love, to allow the subtle body to settle into the gross physical body in a loving way.

We love somebody as long as that person does what we say. A mother says, 'I loved my daughter so deeply till she married somebody who was not of my choice.' Is this love? It is slavery to one's ego. As long as the daughter was an extension of her mother's personality, she felt love for the daughter. This is because, as of now, our love is actually lust which is only violence; deeply rooted violence. It may not be obvious; it may be subtle, but it is there. To own another person, to conquer another person while she resists, is war! Add friendliness to your relationship! Welcome and not just accept the partner as she is. Welcome and accept your own mind, body and being as it is.

You might think that you are very friendly with your own body. No, you are not. If you watch carefully, you will see that you disrespect and abuse your body. You stay up and watch television even if your body cries out for sleep. You keep on eating food even if your stomach is full. You smoke even if your lungs cry out. You drink till you are almost unconscious. Your body is a garbage dump. We are like the pigs that push their noses into filth when they don't want to smell the filth. We torture our bodies for what we feel is 'our enjoyment'.

We are so bothered about terrorism that happens outside. We ignore the violence at home and the violence against our own bodies. Sadism and masochism do not bother us like terrorism does. We torture ourselves with guilt; we torture others with our perfectionism.

A man once told me, 'My wife is a lawyer'. I asked him, 'Does she go to the courts?' The man replied, 'No master, she argues at home!'

Drop your imagination and dreams. Add friendliness towards yourself and others, towards their body, mind and being. Carry words with you that heal others. Carry your body in a way that it heals others. Carry friendliness with you always. This is a spiritual process. Carry the grace and goodwill of Lakshmi (the Goddess of wealth) with you, instead of observing fasts and offering *puja*. Worshipping Lakshmi is alright, but the key is to *become* Lakshmi!

The first time you make an attempt to approach others with your friendliness, they may not receive you openly because of your past behavior. Persist and persevere. Don't stop even if others do not respond to the change in you. Carry on till others believe you and respond.

Drop all imagination about your body, mind and being, and others' body, mind and being; add friendliness towards yourself and others; persevere. Lust will turn to love. Your being will be in eternal bliss.

Appendix

About Paramahamsa Nithyananda

It was under the glow of the spiritual magnet Arunachala in the energy center of Tiruvannamalai in South India, that Nithyananda was born - as Rajasekharan, to Arunachalam and Lokanayaki on 1 January, 1978. The family astrologer predicted that he would be a king amongst holy men.

At the age of 3, Nithyananda was associated with Yogiraj Raghupati Maharaj, a yoga guru who took him through rigorous training and prepared his body, with apparent foresight into the energy explosion that was going to happen in the young body.

From the age of 5, Nithyananda took to deity worship with great passion. He showed profound commitment to the rituals he practiced with the deities. Just a few years later, he came in touch with Mataji Kuppammal, a deeply pious lady who initiated him into *Vedanta* and *Tantra* and started his scriptural learning at that young age. Encountering many mystics from the town of Tiruvannamalai, he received esoteric teachings from them.

At the age of 12, he had his first deep spiritual experience: while sitting on a rock on the Arunachala hillock, he suddenly had a 360 degree panoramic vision, and experienced becoming one

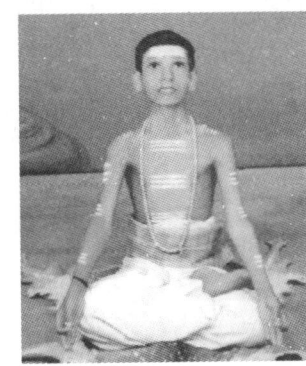

The earliest picture of Paramahamsa in meditation taken when he was 10 years old

with everything around him. This experience further inspired him to forge ahead in his journey inwards.

Academics at school and polytechnic came naturally for Nithyananda. With only the attention he gave in classes, he passed all his grades with distinction. He obtained a diploma degree in Mechanical Engineering from a leading private Polytechnic in Tamilnadu.

Paramahamsa meditating in Arunachala

At the age of 17, he left home driven by the irresistible urge to jump into the real life that he was seeking. He wandered through the length and breadth of India and Nepal, studying Eastern metaphysical sciences and meeting many masters and mystics. He visited many great shrines, ranging from the Himalayas in the North, to Kanyakumari in the South, from Dwaraka in the West to Ganga Sagar in the East. After enduring intense meditation and other austerities, he attained eternal inner bliss...the state of *nithyananda*. At the age of 22, Rajasekharan became Paramahamsa Nithyananda.

Guided by Divine Vision, on Jan. 2003, Parahamamsa set up his mission headquarters in Bangalore, India, in the

Flagging off construction at the mission site

land of mystical and sacred banyan tree.

Today, Nithyananda is an inspiring personality for millions of people worldwide. From his experience of the Truth he has formulated and makes available the Technology of Bliss to every individual. His methods empower us to be physically and mentally fit, with sound spiritual strength in both the inner and outer worlds. Millions of people around the world have experienced radical transformation through his techniques in short periods of time.

Nithyananda gives the tools to live a creative and productive life, guided by intuition and intelligence, rather than by intellect or instinct. He shows the way to excellence in the outer world and radiance in the inner world at the same time. His programs guide one to fall into the natural space known as meditation.

He says, 'Meditation is the master key that can bring success in the material world, and deep fulfillment in your space within.' His powerful techniques and processes that comprise the meditative programs help the flowering and expansive explosion of the individual consciousness.

Paramahamsa Nithyananda cooperates with scientists and researchers the world over, to record mystic phenomena through scientific data. He intrigues the world of medical science with results from his own neurological system. From the astounding observations, scientists feel that the potential for altering the rates and progression of diseases like heart ailments, cancer, arthritis, alcoholism, etc. are beginning to look achievable.

Sacred banyan tree, Bidadi ashram, India

About Nithyananda Mission

Nithyananda Mission is Nithyananda's worldwide movement for meditation and transformation. Established in the year 2003, the Mission continues to transform humanity through transformation of the individual.

Nithyananda Mission ashrams and centers worldwide serve as spiritual laboratories where inner growth is profound and outer growth is a natural consequence. These academies are envisioned to be a place and space to explore and explode, through a host of activities, from meditation to science. They offer Quantum Spirituality, where material and spiritual worlds merge and create blissful living; where creative intelligence stems from deep consciousness.

Hyderabad ashram, India

Nithyananda Dhyanapeetam is the spiritual wing that takes care of the spiritual activities of the mission.

Many projects are in development at the various academies worldwide; and new academies are being

Los Angeles ashram, USA

Seattle ashram, USA

established to provide services in varied fields to humanity at large.

A diverse range of meditation programs and social services are offered worldwide through the Foundation. Free energy healing through the Nithya Spiritual Healing system, free education to youth, encouragement to art and culture, satsangs (spiritual circles), personality development programs, corporate programs, free medical camps and eye surgeries, free meals at all ashrams worldwide, a one-year free residential spiritual training program in India called the Life Bliss Technology, an in-house *Gurukul* system of learning for children, and many more services are offered around the world.

Salem ashram, India

Ananda Sevaks of the Nithya Dheera Seva Sena (NDSS) volunteer force comprising growing numbers of dedicated volunteers around the world, support the mission with great enthusiasm.

Columbus ashram, Ohio, USA

Offerings from Life Bliss Foundation (LBF)

Life Bliss Foundation is the teachings wing of Nithyananda Mission that offers specialized meditation programs worldwide, to benefit millions of people at the levels of body, mind and spirit. A few of them are listed below:

Life Bliss Program Level 1 - Ananda Spurana Program (LBP Level 1 - ASP)

- Energize yourself

A *chakra* workout program that relaxes and energizes the seven major *chakras* in your system. It gives clear intellectual and experiential understanding of your various emotions - greed, fear, worry, attention need, stress, jealousy, ego, discontentment etc. It is designed to create a spiritual effect at the physical level. It is a guaranteed life solution to experience the reality of your own bliss. It is a highly effective workshop, testified by millions of people around the globe.

Life Bliss Program Level 2 - Nithyananda Spurana Program (LBP Level 2 - NSP)

- Death demystified!

A program that unleashes the art of living by demystifying the concept of death. If you know the process and purpose of death, you will live your life in an entirely different way! It creates the space to detach from ingrained and unconscious emotions like guilt, pleasure and pain, all of which stem from the ultimate fear of death. It is a gateway to a new life driven by natural intelligence and spontaneous enthusiasm.

Life Bliss Program Level 3 - Atma Spurana Program (LBP Level 3 - ATSP)

- Connect with your Self!

This is a breakthrough program that analyzes clearly the workings of the mind and shows you experientially how to be the master of the mind rather than let it rule over you. It involves the whole tremendous intellectual understanding coupled with novel meditations to produce instant experiential understanding.

Life Bliss Technology (LBT)

Life Bliss Technology (LBT) is a one-year residential program for youth aged between 18 and 30 years of age, on practical life skills. With its roots in the Eastern system of Vedic education, this program is designed to empower modern youth with good physical, mental and emotional health. By nurturing creative intelligence and spontaneity, and imparting vocational skills, it creates economically and spiritually self-sufficient youth.

Above all, it offers a lifetime opportunity to live and learn under the tutelage of an enlightened Master!

Nithya Spiritual Healing

- Healing through Cosmic energy

A unique and powerful means of healing through the Cosmic energy, this is a meditation for the healer and a means to get healed for the recipient of the healing. Nithyananda continues to initiate thousands of Nithya Spiritual Healers worldwide into this scientific and time-tested healing technique which has healed millions of people of ailments ranging from migraine to cancer.

Nithya Dhyaan
- *Life Bliss Meditation*

Become one among the millions who walk on planet Earth – Un-clutched! Register online and get initiated.

Nithya Dhyaan is a powerful everyday meditation prescribed by Nithyananda to humanity at large. It is a formula or a technique, which is holistic and complete. It works on the entire being to transform it and make it ready for the ultimate experience of enlightenment to dawn. Each segment of this technique complements the remaining segments to help raise the individual consciousness. It trains you to un-clutch from your mind and live a blissful life. It is the meditation for Eternal Bliss.

If you wish to be initiated into Nithya Dhyaan, you may visit http://www.dhyanapeetam.org and register online. You will receive through mail, a *mala*, bracelet, a spiritual name given by Nithyananda for your own spiritual growth (optional), Nithya Dhyaan Meditation CD and Nithya Dhyaan booklet in a language of your choice, personally signed by Nithyananda (mention your choice in the comment column).

Nithyananda says, 'My advent on planet Earth is to create a new cycle of individual consciousness causing Collective Consciousness to enter the Superconscious zone.'

To achieve this,

Hundred thousand people will be initiated to live as *Jeevan Muktas* – liberated beings experiencing 'living enlightenment', and 1 billion people will be initiated into Nithya Dhyaan – Life Bliss Meditation – designed to cause a shift in the individual consciousness on planet Earth.

Contact us

Nithyananda Dhyanapeetam is the wing of Nithyananda Mission that handles the spiritual activities of the mission. Listed below are the main Vedic temples and Nithyananda Mission ashrams world wide.

USA:

Los Angeles
Los Angeles Vedic Temple
9720 Central Avenue, Montclair,
CA 91763
USA
Ph.: 1-909-625-1400
Email: programs@lifebliss.org
URL: www.lifebliss.org

Los Angeles Ashram
928 Huntington Dr,
Duarte, Los Angeles
CA 91010
Ph.: 1-626-205-3286

San Jose

San Jose Vedic Temple
5788 Riochester Ct.
San Jose CA 95123
Ph.: 510-573-3433, 510-813-6474

Florida
Orlando Vedic Temple &
International Vedic Hindu University
113 N. Econlockhatchee Trail, Orlando
Florida, 32825
Ph.: 626-272-4043

New York
Queens Vedic Temple
129-10 Liberty Avenue, Richmond Hill,
Queens NY 11420
Ph.: 718-296-1995

Ohio
Ohio Vedic Temple & Ashram
820 Pollock Rd,
Delaware, Ohio
Ph: 740-362-2046

Oklahoma
Oklahoma City Vedic Temple
3048 N. Grand Blvd.
Oklahoma city
OK 73107
Ph.: 405-833-6107

Missouri
St Louis Vedic Temple
12555 Sunset Dr.
St Louis, MO. 63128
Ph.: 314-849-6760

Washington
Seattle Vedic Temple
2877 152nd Ave Ne building 13
Redmond Washington 98052
Ph.: 425-591-1010

Phoenix
6605 South 39th Ave,
Phoenix, AZ 85041
Ph.: 480 388 2490
Email: vedictemplephx@yahoo.com

Malaysia
Klang Ashram
No 62, Jalan Serempang Dua,
Off Jalan Sungai Betek,
Taman Betek Indah,
41400 Klang, Malaysia

INDIA
Bangalore, Karnataka
(Spiritual headquarters. Vedic Temple located here)
Nithyananda Dhyanapeetam
Nithyanandapuri
Kallugopahalli
Mysore Road, Bidadi
Bangalore - 562 109
Karnataka
Ph.: +91+80 65591844 / 27202084
Email: mail@nithyananda.org
URL:www.nithyananda.org

Hosur, Karnataka
Nithyanandapuri,
Kanuka Estate
Nallur post,
Hosur - 635 109
Krishnagiri District,
Tamilnadu
Ph.: 99947 77898 / 99443 21809

Hyderabad, Andhra Pradesh
Sri Anandeshwari Temple,
Nithyananda Giri,
Pashambanda Sathamrai Village
Shamshabad Mandal
Rangareddy District - 501 218
Andhra Pradesh
Ph.: 91 +84132 60311 / 60044
Mob.: 98665 00350 / 93964 82358

Salem, Tamil Nadu
Nithyanandapuri
102, Azhagapurampudur
Salem – 636 016
Tamilnadu
Ph.: +91 94433 64644 / 94432 35262
(Behind Sharada College)

Namakkal, Tamil Nadu
Nithyanandapuri,
2/200, Tirumangkuruchi Post,
Namakkal – 637003
Tamilnadu, INDIA
Ph.: +91 +94433 88437

Tiruvannamalai, Tamil Nadu
Nithyanandapuri,
Othaivaadai street,
Pavazhakundru,
Tiruvannamalai - 606 601,
Tamil Nadu

Tiruvannamalai, Tamil Nadu
Nithyanandapuri,
Opposite Rajarajeswari Temple
Girivalam path
Tiruvannamalai
Ph.: 94449 91089 / 94432 33789

Tiruvannamalai, Tamil Nadu
Arunachala Dhyanapeetam
Keel Katcharappattu Village
Tiruvannamalai
Ph.: 94449 91089 / 94432 33789

Pattanam, Tamil Nadu
Nithyanandapuri, Puthupatti road,
Pattanam
Rasipuram (Taluk) - 605602
Namakkal disrict
Ph.: 04287 222842

Rajapalayam, Tamilnadu
Nithyanandapuri,
Kothainachiarpuram,
Rajapalayam,
Virudhunagar District
Ph.: 04563 260002 / 94426 23768

Pondicherry, Tamilnadu
Nithyanandapuri,
Embalam to Villianoor main road,
Embalam post,
Pondicherry - 605 106
Ph.: 94420 36037 / 97876 67604

Poompuhar Aadeenam, Tamilnadu
Shivarajayoga Mutt
Opposite Poompuhar College
Melayur Post
Seerkaali Taluk
Nagai District - 609 107

Suggested for further reading

- Guaranteed Solutions for sex, fear, worry etc.
- Nithyananda Vol. 1 (The first volume of a biographical account of Nithyananda)
- Life Bliss Program Level 2 - Nithyananda Spurana Program
- Follow me IN! (Life Bliss Program Level 3 - Atma Spurana Program)
- You can Heal (Nithya Spiritual Healing)
- Meditation is for you
- Bliss is the path and the goal
- The only way out is IN
- Rising in love with the Master
- Bhagavad Gita series
- Uncommon answers to common questions
- Open the door...Let the breeze in!

To purchase books and other items, visit www.lifeblissgalleria.com or contact us.

Visit http://www.youtube.com/lifeblissfoundation to view over 400 FREE video discourses of Paramahamsa Nithyananda.